Model Railroads

Above: Christopher Hollingsworth brings a 3½-inch gauge LMS 'Black Five' 4–6–0 at a fast speed through the main station of the Brighouse and Halifax Model Engineering Society's track.

Above center: One of the smallest live-steam locomotives in the world. A Great Western 2-8-0T in OO gauge to a design by Professor Sherwood of Sydney University, Australia.

Above right: Denver & Rio Grande: a 7¼-inch model of K-36 class 2-8-2 No 487.

Below: Near perfection and Great Western – an EM-gauge model of the 'Saint' class 4-6-0 *Saint Dunstan*. It is displayed at the Pendon Museum, Long Wittenham, Oxfordshire, England.

Previous page: Keith Ladbury's Paddington Station – with five platforms instead of 12. A model of the French built 4-4-2 *La France* is leaving the station.

Model
Railroads

Brian Hollingsworth

HAMLYN

London : New York : Sydney : Toronto

A Bison Book

Published by
The Hamlyn Publishing Group
Limited
London New York Sydney
Toronto
Astronaut House, Feltham
Middlesex, England

Produced by
Bison Books Limited
4 Cromwell Place
London SW7

ISBN: 0 600 34944 6

Printed in Spain

Produced by Colourviews
Limited for Bison Books under
the direction of
Patrick Whitehouse

Designer: Adrian Hodgkins

A busy goods yard in OO
gauge, displayed among
many other layouts in the
Peco Modelrama Exhibition
at Beer, Devon, England.
Note the wagons belonging
to private firms, typical of
prewar Britain.

Contents

Introduction

A sizable proportion of the world's male population fancies itself at the building and operating of railroads but, perhaps fortunately, the majority lacks the opportunity to do it in full size. Hence the proliferation of model and miniature systems and the existence of many keen amateurs who build and run these replicas of the real thing. This book is primarily intended to describe and illustrate the current state of the art, but some attention will be given to its history, which is in fact more ancient than that of full-size railroads. It should be no surprise that nearly 200 years ago a model demonstration steam locomotive preceded the first commercial full-size one.

The book attempts to cover the whole range of model railroads in ascending order of size. The range begins with those made to 1:220 scale – here a typical locomotive would weigh about an ounce and be a mere 2½–3 inches long – and ends with 1:2 scale, where each locomotive would weigh several tons. Although, strictly speaking, a model could be full size or even several times full size, such giants of the railroad model world belong elsewhere.

Owing to this wide coverage, from model railroads which will go inside a violin case to those that need a country estate or even planning permission before they can be built, instruction on how to construct model railroads is rather overshadowed by the theoretical possibilities. Some of the many practical instruction books are listed in the bibliography, or mentioned in the text.

A small problem arises because of the difference between the North American and the British names for certain railroad objects. Should we speak of cars, trucks and stacks, or wagons, bogies and chimneys? In fact, whichever name seems most appropriate or convenient is used, the context being relied on to resolve any ambiguity. In any case, more and more either term is used and understood either side of the Atlantic. For example, both Sante Fe and Southern – two of the top United States' railroads – call themselves Railways.

Left: Pinconning & Blind River Railroad 4-6-2 on trestle bridge – 'Shay' geared locomotive below.

1   Running a Railroad

In the 176 years since a Cornishman called Richard Trevithick put the first full-size locomotive on the track, mankind has put perhaps 500,000 more upon the rails. This handsome figure has been quite eclipsed, however, by what has been achieved during the longer period of 196 years since the first model locomotive was built by another man from Cornwall, William Murdoch. Certainly 10 and probably 20 times as many model as full-size trains have left factories and workshops to enter service. So the beginning of model locomotives (in fact, the Murdoch locomotive did not run on rails) came before there were any big ones to copy. It was not to be the last time that model practices were to anticipate full size.

No doubt William Murdoch and his friends built their model as a serious experiment in steam propulsion, but it seems they also had fun running it, scaring the Vicar out of his wits one night, for example. This brings us to the reason for the existence of most model railroads – they are built and run purely for pleasure. Of course, model railroads have been built for serious demonstration purposes and for training but those built for advertising and profit are in fact exploiting their pleasure-giving powers.

So, at the outset it is necessary to declare that, for the purposes of this book, a model railroad is regarded as one which is a fun thing, not built for any directly useful or commercial reason. It should also have running upon it self-propelled trains and efforts should have been made to make reasonable representations – the right number of wheels, for example – of those that did run, or might have run, on the full-size railroads of the world. It is important to set down the boundary lines inside which this work is intended to lie, for example, mere toys are excluded from it, although proper model railroads grew out of them.

Someone might ask whether model railroads ever fulfill a useful function – apart from indirect benefits like earning money by admission charges, providing employment or keeping children out of mischief. In this connection we note (in his book *Most Secret War*), Professor Jones describing how during World War II the fact that a member of his staff had built a coal-fired 1-gauge locomotive got him a hearing with top officers in the Air Force – with the result that the new methods thereby propounded significantly reduced bomber casualties. Knowledge obtained through building model railroads can help more directly by providing a technical background and at least the elements of the way electricity works.

Right: Paddington Station 'throat' on Keith Ladbury's Great Western Railway model in OO gauge.

Below: A view of Madderport on John Ahern's classic Madder Valley Railway. Note the fantastic attention to detail among the buildings and such things as the horse bus and the lady with a baby carriage.

Most interesting is the way in which model railroads break down social and class barriers. I once saw an ingenious plastic toy railroad being demonstrated on the floor beside a duty-free shop in Jan Smuts Airport, Johannesburg. The little group that gathered round enjoyed the demonstration together, laughing and smiling, quite forgetting their usual strict divisions into whites and blacks, crew and passengers, customs officials and the public.

Although a little train buzzing round a circle is fun for a time, the best way to continue enjoying a model railroad is to have a theme for it. This gives a layout originality and individuality and it is quite independent of such qualities as complexity, cost, size, technical achievements or absolute fidelity to the prototype. All these other things are now available for the asking at reasonable prices, off the shelves of any model shop, but originality and individuality come out of ourselves when we create the make-believe world of our own model railroad.

Great things have been done in this way in the past. If you have never climbed the Madderhorn, take the Madder Valley Railway train (John Ahern's enchanting model is now preserved in Pendon Railway Museum, Long Wittenham, near Oxford, England) to Gammon Worthy Halt and follow the directions in the Guide Book. There is also the legendary land of Lyonesse, taken from Arthurian legend and sited off the western tip of England; it is as infested with railroads as the meadows of New Jersey. Perhaps, too, you never knew that Dylan Thomas' immortal village of Llareggub had a line (David Rowe's Milkwood Railway) that matched the quaintness and charm of its inhabitants, many of whom can be seen in its streets.

The other approach is to use quite different qualities – in fact, reducing imagination to an absolute minimum.

Left: The President's business car on the Bangor & Machias Railroad.

Right: A near-exact re-creation of a vanished line – a Campbelltown and Machrihanish light railroad train at the quayside. Every detail is modeled as closely as possible on the actual location by Nigel MacMillan in Glasgow.

Below: On3 narrow gauge: Florence & Cripple Creek Railroad 4-6-0 hauling a day coach and combine car, both by Star Models.

Above: The quest for perfection: London & North Eastern Railway 4-6-2 *Papyrus* takes the Queen of Scots Pullman Express round the elegant curves of a fabulous O-gauge layout.

Left: Imagination should run riot: an enchanting railbus sets out from Llysfaen on its way to King's Gap on the narrow-gauge garden layout of William Stocks. His Heatherfield Light Railway is built to gauge-1 scale, running on gauge-O track.

Above right: There must be a story behind everything on your model railroad: in this case when Driver Speedwell arrived at Torreyford from Paddington with the through express to Torreymouth on a recent summer Saturday, he was in charge of 7013 *Bristol Castle*. He demanded assistance for the North Devonshire banks as he had 16 fully loaded coaches behind the tender. No 7902 *Eaton Mascot Hall* was hurriedly provided as pilot and as a result the fitters did not have time to fix the faulty packing of the gland of the right-hand piston. The photograph shows evidence of this as the tell-tale clouds of steam trailed behind 7902 when the two engines worked the heavy train up to speed on the first of the 1-in-100 gradients of the NDR.

This is to try and bring back to miniature life, with the highest possible fidelity of detail some long-lost delight of the railroad world. Do such names as Rio Grande Southern, Sandy River & Rangely Lakes, Salzkammergut Lokalbahn, Lynton & Barnstaple or Leek & Manifold mean anything to you? Or perhaps there is a lost or once-great line, depot or station in your own home town? So, in the basic thinking behind your model railroad, for the imagination of a novelist you may have to substitute the painstaking patience of an archeolo-gist or historical researcher. A little less demanding is a layout which is intended to show with fidelity the flavor of some real railroad rather than an actual replica of some part of it. At Pendon Railway Museum, one notes such details as the correct red roses in the buttonholes of HO-gauge Great Western travelling ticket collectors.

Some model railroads ape full-size ones in habits as well as aspect. The Model Railroad Club of Union, New Jersey, United States, for example, not only runs no

Right: Running your own railroad: a private world where you and you only are the boss. This relatively humble example shows how, in a simple shed, very satisfying results can be achieved.

Next page: The Great Western scene – the excellent effect of using proprietary equipment is demonstrated by this view of the OO-gauge layout built by Keith Ladbury.

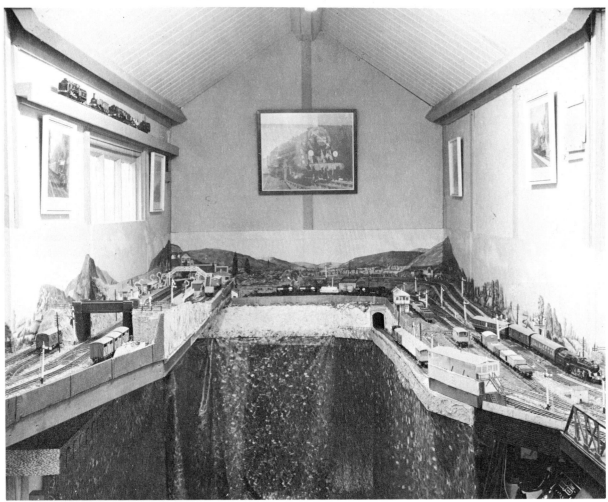

train except when properly scheduled or called, but no car may be moved without a miniature waybill. If taken really seriously, timetable operation can be excellent fun even when the railroad is only a toy one. It is usual for the clocks which govern the working to run several times as fast as normal ones as it is really better to spend only an afternoon or an evening on a full day's timetable.

Yet a further approach is to attempt to portray or represent some particular facet of railroad operation in extreme perfection; while at the same time, since life is short, taking what comes elsewhere. John Wettern's Petts Wood Railway in Croydon, Surrey, England, for example, had locomotives that were basically cardboard boxes and rolling stock with printed paper sides; but the three stations were fully signalled with both mechanical and electrical interlocking according to the strictest interpretation of the Ministry of Transport requirements. When, in due time, some replicas of the elegant umber motive power of the London Brighton & South Coast Railway arrived, something almost seemed to have been lost.

An extreme example of this kind of thing is the cult of live steam using the bigger gauges of 3½ inches and above. Here the locomotives are not only often modelled down to the last rivet, but also have real coal fires making steam inside them. On the other hand, the tracks are usually absurd affairs on stilts, while the rolling stock, being designed to carry drivers and passengers 12 or 16 times scale size, is also as unrealistic as could be.

Above: Original thinking in model railroads: a 7mm scale 49mm (almost 2-inch) gauge model of the Great Western broad-gauge single-wheeler *Actaeon* by William Salter.

Below: Enjoy model railroads on the grand scale: both observer and driver-fireman anticipate with pleasure the coming 13-mile run from Hythe to Dungeness on the 15-inch gauge Romney, Hythe & Dymchurch Railway in Kent, England.

Right: Aberystwyth Station, Wales on the OO-gauge layout belonging to Keith Ladbury.

2 The Development of Model Railroading

When did the first model railroad open? One candidate is illustrated here – enchanting little *Topsy* and her figure-of-eight track of $3\frac{1}{8}$-inch gauge, dating from around 1870. This train set was built by a man called William Williams, the works foreman of the first narrow-gauge public railroad in the world, for Charles Spooner, the general manager. It returned a few years ago to the Festiniog Railway and is now displayed in the museum at Porthmadog, North Wales. The outfit is typical of the few model railroads around at this period, in that it was built to order by a craftsman of considerable skill who had no choice but to work from first principles and basic raw materials. 'Live steam' coal-burning steam locomotive models in gauges from $1\frac{3}{4}$–15 inches are still being individually made (in ever increasing numbers too) in a similar fashion, although usually to established gauges, scales and standards.

During this period commercial toy trains began to appear in the shops. In the account of their progression to the model trains we know today Germany, and especially the name of the South German town of Nuremberg, recurs with monotonous frequency. Günterman of Nuremberg introduced self-propulsion by a clockwork mechanism in 1855, Issmayer sold train sets with curved rails in 1866, while in 1882 Plank offered electric drive. Maerklin, who still make trains in West Germany, in 1892 offered a still grateful public the standards from which our present ones eventually developed. These were gauge numbers 1, 2 and 3 (effectively $1\frac{3}{4}$, 2 and $2\frac{1}{2}$ inches). A year or two later Maerklin introduced the immortal O gauge ($1\frac{1}{4}$-inch) which was to dominate the model railroad scene on both sides of the Atlantic until after World War II.

At this time the first non-German name comes into the picture – that of W J Bassett-Lowke of Northampton, England. His idea was that it was not enough for a toy

Below: *Topsy* ran on one of the first model railroads ever. She was built in the Festiniog Railway Company's shops by the works foreman.

Left: Typical of the model locomotives of the Victorian age is this charming live-steam 2-4-0.

Left: *Topsy* returns to the Festiniog Railway. Chairman Alan Pegler unwraps her on 4 August 1963.

locomotive just to have one wheel at each corner; he thought it should have measurements and physical features which corresponded at least to some extent with those of a particular full-size machine. The simple lines and bright colors of British full-size trains (themselves regarded as toys by the rest of the world) made it easier to take this important step. Inevitably, he got a Nurnberger to make them for him. Bassett-Lowke co-operated with the firm founded by one Stefan Bing to produce a range of scale models with steam, electric and clockwork drive, that represented a golden age. Survivors from these days are now sold at Christies' of London, the top auctioneers of the antique trade; but unfortunately Bing was Jewish and his firm did not survive the Nazi period.

Maerklin and others, including Ives and Lionel of the United States, included models that were more than toys in their ranges, but toys were predominant. The main process used was lithographed (preprinted) pressed tin plate – 'tin trains' said the irreverent, but 'made from best tinned steel plate' said the catalogues. This process lent itself to mass production and consequently low prices. Production runs of 100,000 and more for one particular model were common. An engineer called Henry Greenly was Bassett-Lowke's technical consultant (as he would now be called) in these developments. Greenly was responsible in 1909 for starting the first periodical – *Models, Railways and Locomotives* – devoted to the hobby. Although Greenly's effort did not survive World War I, it was a worthy forerunner of the numerous magazines which guide and inform the enthusiast today.

Another development that came along during this period, which doubtless began in a quite informal and unrecorded way, was the formation of model railroad clubs. Like-minded people could combine their re-

19

sources and skills and so between them create something far superior to that possible to them as individuals. It is noted that The Model Railway Club of London was founded in 1910, but it has developed more as a forum for exchange of ideas rather than for providing a layout. In contrast is The Model Railroad Club of Union, New Jersey, previously mentioned, which has in hand a layout 40 feet by 40 feet in extent, intended to contain 50 scale miles of HO-gauge track. An extension of 40 feet by 150 feet (with 165 scale miles of track) is planned, together with large O and N-gauge layouts in addition to meeting rooms, a shop and bar.

After World War I people with smaller houses wanted model railroads and so demand rose for the smaller sizes of model train. Accordingly, gauges 2 and 3 almost disappeared from model-shop shelves and even 1 gauge became special. O gauge became the norm and dominated the hobby in a great period.

It is even possible to find working layouts from that period surviving over 50 years later. Norman Eagles' O gauge Sherwood Forest Section of the London, Midland and Scottish Railway (better known as 'Crewchester') is such a one; it is certainly a candidate for being the oldest surviving working model railroad in the world. It features clockwork traction, and this supposedly antiquated method of propulsion matches up to electricity in a surprisingly satisfactory way.

This need for smaller-sized model trains led in 1923 to the introduction of what is now the dominant gauge of the model-railroad world, 'half-O' or HO, with a track gauge of approximately $\frac{5}{8}$ of an inch, half that of O gauge. Bing for Bassett-Lowke produced the famous 'Table-Top Railway' in that size, designed by the great Henry Greenly. As forerunners of the largest locomotive fleet the world has ever known, these little clockwork and electric Bing 2-4-0s and 2-4-0Ts just

Left: Early tin-plate scale models: Carette of Nuremberg made this travelling post-office van. It was capable of both picking up and dropping mail bags at speed as per the prototype.

Above left: Bing of Nuremberg produced this O-gauge Great Northern Railway of England 4-4-2 before World War I.

Above: Hornby begins moving from toys to scale models: a true-to-type Great Western *County of Bedford* in a rather toy-like environment.

(debatably) scraped from being mere toys into the model category.

Of course, around this period there were able individuals to whom the difficulties of making tiny electric motors from scratch were just a worthwhile challenge. In due course some of them went into business on a small scale – names such as Holtzappfel, Bond's and Stewart Reidpath come to mind – so that people who could manage to cut out and solder some metal into a good representation of a superstructure (but who found microscopic electric motors beyond them) could go ahead and build themselves tiny locomotives. Track was fabricated by soldering brass strips, say $\frac{1}{16}$ of an inch wide by $\frac{1}{8}$ of an inch high, to form the rails to others, say $\frac{1}{8}$ of an inch wide by $\frac{1}{16}$ of an inch thick, to form the sleepers. Electric power was led to the locomotives via a conductor rail soldered to wood screws driven into the baseboard; soon correct section brass rail became available. The high priest of the 'do-it-yourself-with-solder' era in Britain was a clergyman called Edward Beal whose text books (*Railway Modelling in Miniature, The Craft of Railway Modelling* and others) contain much that is entirely valid today, particularly in their emphasis on non-railroad accessories for model railroads such as houses, factories and shops.

Also wholly valid, active and commercially well-supported even today is the Beal approach of building a whole model railroad from scratch – in fact 'scratch-building' is the term used – using basic materials and a few helpful manufactured parts to create replicas of everything in, on or around a railroad.

The parts and materials to make a model are often offered conveniently boxed as a kit, usually complete with instructions. The date of the first one is obscure but it seems that kits were quite common in North America even before World War II.

The American firm of Dorfan from Newark, New Jersey, was responsible for introducing the process of pressure die casting during the 1920s. A single molding could now produce a locomotive body complete to the last scale rivet. The result was very satisfying, although not in those early days comparable with fabrication by hand. The technique spread rapidly and now dominates mass-produced model locomotive construction. Of course, it had been in use earlier for the production of small details needed in large numbers such as chairs for scale bullhead track.

In the 1920s electric drive began to take the lion's share of model motive power duties, but it held one substantial drawback. This was the unwelcome and unrealistic presence of a side or center conductor rail on railroads that purported to be totally steam operated. The bold idea of using the two running rails for the two

conductors and insulating the wheels of all rolling stock is thought to have originated in the United States. Firms such as Mantua and Varney certainly offered two-rail commercially in the 1930s, but outside the USA the system (now virtually universal) was practically unknown before World War II.

Another great step forward was the founding of The National Model Railway Association in the United States during September 1935. This body was dedicated to the advancement of the hobby, in the first place by laying down a set of mandatory standards for track and wheels. Currently there are 27,000 members domiciled in all five continents.

One sad event around this time (but which had pleasant results for model buffs) was the demise of certain beloved 2-foot gauge railroads on both sides of the Atlantic. FJ Roche marked the event with models of a Baldwin-built 2-4-2T and Manning Wardle 2-6-2T, from the Lynton & Barnstaple Railway of England. These were to the same *scale* as normal O-gauge models but made to run on HO-gauge track. Complete layouts in this style, such as the surviving Madder Valley Railway, were the forerunners of what is now a cult, well supported by the model trade.

Plastic moldings for rolling stock – again now a near-universal method – were introduced by the Leeds Model Company of Yorkshire, England, in 1937, just before the world settled down for a period to more serious things than toy trains. From radar development during World War II came much better magnets for locomotive mechanisms, both more permanent and more potent; hence smaller motors more easily installed in scale body work and the tiresome process of re-magnetization was redundant. All this gave a great fillip to HO and OO gauges and opened the way to even smaller sizes in due course. Better glues were another wartime spin-off, this time from aircraft construction.

During those bitter years development was confined to those able to keep clear of the conflict. One notes an Irishman called CL Fry perfecting the generation of

synchronized smoke puffs from the chimneys of his electrically-driven steam locomotives of his superb Irish International Railways and Tramway layout.

So it will be seen that, when in 1946 the world began again to think of diversion rather than destruction, practically all the elements of model railroading as we know it today were already there for the taking – except one. This was electronics, and here the revolution – for revolution it is – is in our midst right now.

One of the earliest applications of electronic-type circuits to model railroads was the use of high-frequency (HF) current for train lighting. This was superimposed on the direct current (DC) which drove the trains. These two types of current could easily be separated on the locomotives and cars. If the high-frequency current was then used for lighting the lights themselves would not dim when the train slowed down, or go out when it stopped as they would do if the lighting circuits were directly connected. This development was typical of all the subsequent applications of electronics to model railroads in that it was aimed at increasing realism. On most real trains, after all, the lights do not go out when the train stops.

Something very much akin to this system was used by the group who were the first to show the ultimate weapon in the fight for realism – a layout run by controlled live-steam locomotives to exhibition standards. This took place at Manchester, England, in 1965 (see Chapter 9). Since then electrically controlled live steam has been offered commercially, with butane gas firing. Curiously enough model live steam, although it works like the prototype (and this is very important), does not produce very realistic sounds. The little fire chariots chuff, but the timbre of big steam is missing. Since the sound of the exhaust and other noises of steam locomotives are one of their principal charms, this is a pity. Sound has been a preoccupation of model makers for many years and, even before the war, toy-train manufacturers (Lionel of the United States was early in the field) made engines that chuffed. Whistles and so on could also be sounded, but not by the use of steam.

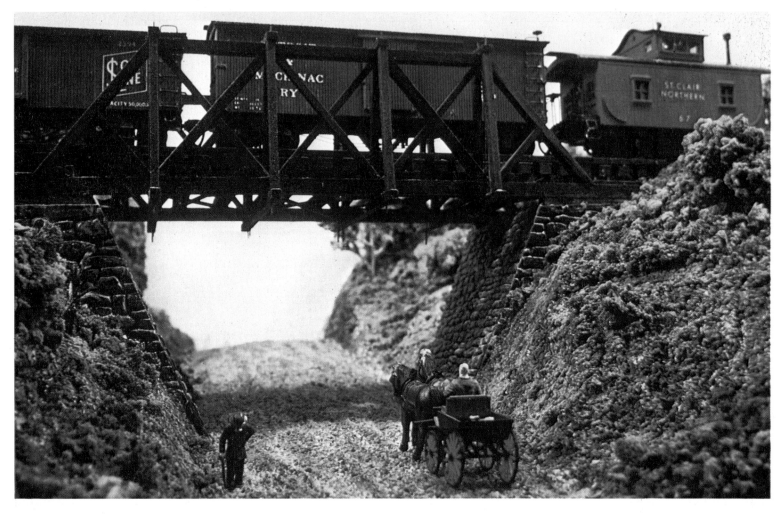

Above: The rail end of a freight crosses a sunken road on Irv Schultz' HO-gauge St Clair Northern Railroad, St Clair Shores, Michigan.

Left: Bangor Engine Yard: scratchbuilt coaling tower with the sandhouse in the foreground.

Right: A view of the turntable and locomotive facility on St Clair Northern Railroad.

Next page: What is still by far the largest model railroad in the world was opened in 1927. This view shows New Romney Station, on the 13-mile 15-inch gauge Romney, Hythe & Dymchurch Railway shortly after opening.

In 1965 a group of members of the Puget Sound Model Railroad Club produced (and described in the *Model Railroader* magazine) a system whereby a minute loud-speaker, small enough to fit into an HO-gauge locomotive tender, could be fed with sounds generated 'on shore' as it were. The steam sound was modulated on the locomotive by a contact which opened and closed as the locomotive moved. Thus, 'choo-choo' noises were properly synchronized with the wheels. Bells and whistle signals could be sounded to order as if produced on the locomotive. Again, commercial availability is now a reality, although high cost precludes many people from having the device.

Another rather unrealistic feature of the average model railroad was the fact that, when you shut off power, the model train stops dead in a few inches, while a real one would coast for a mile or two. Electronic circuits were introduced which allowed the power to die away gradually; how gradually would depend on the setting of a control lever which effectively simulated the brake lever of a real locomotive, enabling model

'hoggers' to 'wipe the clock' when required, in true railroad fashion. ('Hogger' and 'wipe the clock' are railroad terms for engineers [drivers] and 'apply emergency braking' respectively.) This feature has now become common. Again, do-it-yourself instruction (*Model Railroader*, 1960) preceded its availability in model shops by several years.

For some time previously the best locomotive electric mechanisms had inertia added rather than simulated by the addition of a flywheel to the armature shaft. Neither this nor electronic inertia, however, did anything to improve the lack of realism of switching (shunting) operations on a model layout. First, watch a switcher give a cut of cars a kick and see them coast easily through the siding switch and run on; then go home and try it on your own layout. Even with the best of bearings on the model cars the results are pathetic. The simple addition of flywheels to the axles (described in chapter 14) can greatly reduce this gap between the way a car coasts in model form and the way it does in full size.

Right: A 'Dean Goods' 0-6-0 crosses a representation of the famous swing bridge across the Mawddach Estuary at Barmouth, Wales.

Below: Buildings German-style by Faller.

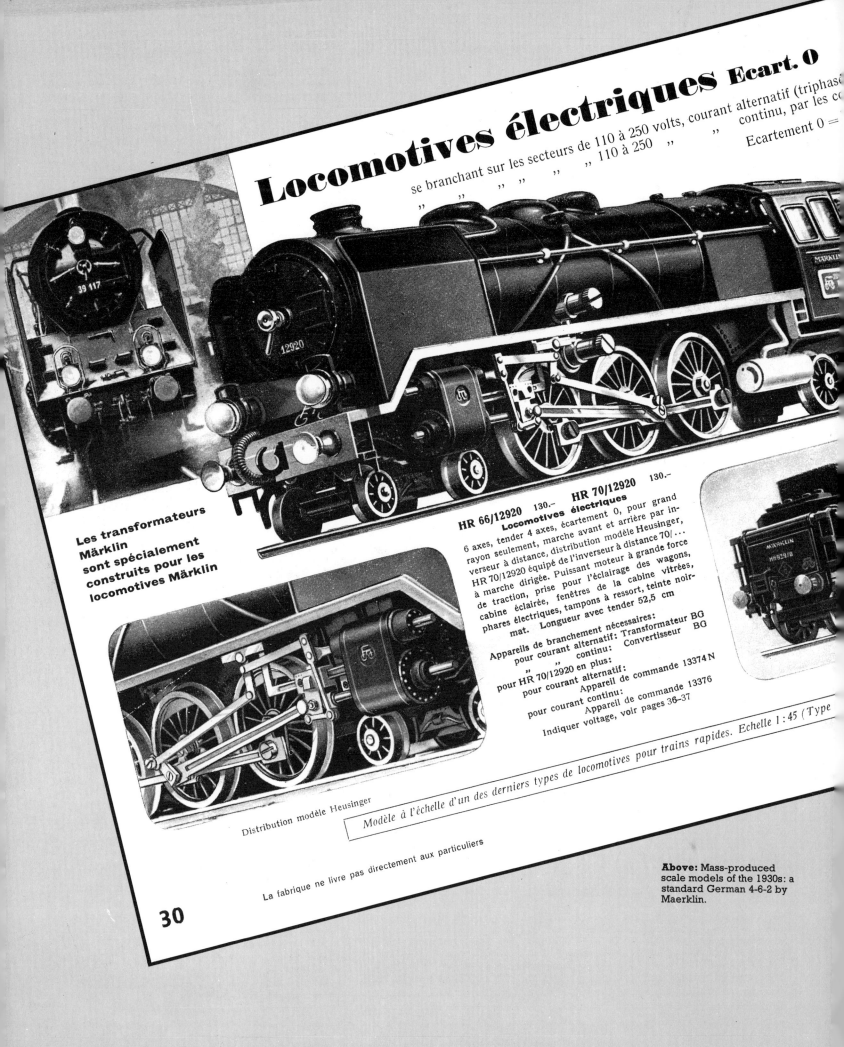

Locomotives électriques Ecart. 0

se branchant sur les secteurs de 110 à 250 volts, courant alternatif (triphasé
" " " " 110 à 250 " continu, par les c...

Ecartement 0 =

Les transformateurs Märklin sont spécialement construits pour les locomotives Märklin

HR 66/12920 130.–   **HR 70/12920** 130.–
Locomotives électriques

6 axes, tender 4 axes, écartement 0, pour grand rayon seulement, marche avant et arrière par inverseur à distance, distribution modèle Heusinger, HR 70/12920 équipé de l'inverseur à distance 70/... à marche dirigée. Puissant moteur à grande force de traction, prise pour l'éclairage des wagons, cabine éclairée, fenêtres de la cabine vitrées, phares électriques, tampons à ressort, teinte noir-mat. Longueur avec tender 52,5 cm

Appareils de branchement nécessaires:
pour courant alternatif: Transformateur BG
" continu: Convertisseur BG
pour HR 70/12920 en plus:
pour courant alternatif:
Appareil de commande 13374 N
pour courant continu:
Appareil de commande 13376
Indiquer voltage, voir pages 36–37

Distribution modèle Heusinger

Modèle à l'échelle d'un des derniers types de locomotives pour trains rapides. Echelle 1 : 45 (Type

Modèle à l'échelle d'un des derniers types de locomotives

30

Above: Mass-produced scale models of the 1930s: a standard German 4-6-2 by Maerklin.

The ultimate in electronic control is provided by a computerized system now being introduced by numerous firms on both sides of the Atlantic. In addition to setting up the simulated inertia effects just described, several individual locomotives on the same circuit can be separately controlled. The actual control is done by an electronic chip in each locomotive, which responds to digital messages sent from the controllers.

Until now, if more than one locomotive was run, a layout had to be divided into numerous separate electrical sections, with complicated switching, and all sorts of difficulties arose when trains ran from one electrical section to another. Operations involving any co-operation between two locomotives, such as backing one on to another to form a double-header, were quite impossible. So yet another bastion falls in this search for realism.

A particularly annoying bugbear of the conventional layout is the need for surgical cleanliness of wheel treads and rails. This is because electricity requires 30,000 volts per inch to jump a gap. In the model world, where a nominal 12 volts is normal, a gap of more than say $1/2000$ of an inch between wheel and rail causes an involuntary and embarrassing stop. A British firm called Relco are offering a modest piece of electronics – literally a black box – which superimposes a special high-frequency oscillation on the normal voltage when current ceases to flow. This has the effect of burning off the dirt as trains run, in a quite remarkable manner. In this way one of the most trying annoyances of model railroading passes into history.

Conventional developments since the war have included the introduction of ever smaller commercial sizes and an ever greater (and now quite extraordinary) variety of prototype in the older sizes, particularly HO/OO. These range from Stephenson's *Rocket* to diesel and electric trains so new that they have only just been introduced in full size. Old scales such as 1 and even 3 have returned and in almost all ways railroad modellers have never had so much choice.

Perhaps the last word rests with the Indiana Central College of Indianapolis, USA. This establishment has just begun offering a higher education course in model railroading practice and theory. So much for a hobby that used to be considered too childish for grown men.

Below: Large-scale model railroads: Bassett-Lowke's 4-4-2 *Little Giant*, designed by Henry Greenly, was the first scale model to run on the 15-inch gauge.

3   Gauges, Scales and Standards

It has been said that authors who try and explain things to others usually underestimate their readers' intelligence while overestimating their previous knowledge. Accordingly two simple definitions are in order.

First, the gauge of a railroad is defined as the distance between the inner or 'running' edges of the rails. It is usual to specify a nominal gauge and allow small discrepancies. Track can be slightly 'wide-to-gauge,' within strict limits, either through some fault (spikes work loose even on the best regulated lines) or are deliberately made so to ease movement on sharp curves.

Second, the scale of a model railroad is defined as the ratio between the dimensions of the model and those of its prototype. Three methods are used to specify the scale. First, one can speak of the fraction of an inch (or in larger sizes, the number of inches) which represents one foot, for example, $\frac{1}{4}$ of an inch to 1 foot. A purer way which is independent of the units used, would be to talk of the proportion between the two sizes; in this case it would be 1:48. This second method applies equally to

metric and imperial measures. The third way, which applies to HO, the commonest scale, is to combine the metric and imperial systems, and talk of so many millimeters to the foot. HO then is specified as 3.5mm to the foot or, for short, 3.5mm scale. This last way of specifying the scale preceded by many years any serious thought of metrication in either Britain or North America.

Even armed with these definitions, this chapter must be regarded as heavy going. This is because George Stephenson chose as the standard gauge for the world's railroads the awkward figure of 4 feet 8½ inches. Consequently, when you make a model to a particular scale, either its gauge comes out to some odd dimension or, if the model gauge is a round number, then the scale has to be peculiar. A third alternative is to have a simple scale and build the locomotive to run on a simple gauge which is, however, not quite the scale equivalent. Sometimes the pioneers did one of these things, sometimes another. Unfortunately, sometimes they did one thing on one side of the English Channel or Atlantic (or, in one notorious case, one side of the United States) and

Left: The 7mm to 1 foot scale O-gauge Great Western Torpoint Railway layout. Handmade perfection by J Harrison.

Below: Three gauges and scales by Maerklin of West Germany: vintage electric in Z gauge or 'mini club' (front), the smallest commercially available size; modern electric in HO gauge (rear); and vintage steam in 1 gauge (center).

another on the other. Hence, two or more scales arose for the same gauge and more than one gauge arose for the same scale, which is very confusing.

One notes from the table given, for example, that 1¼-inch gauge (O gauge) in the United States is used with the strictly incorrect but simple scale of 1:48, or ¼ of an inch to 1 foot, while elsewhere 1:43.5 or 7mm to one foot is used. To make things even more complicated, some O-gauge pundits in the USA work to a scale of 1:45.2 or ¹⁷⁄₆₄ of an inch to 1 foot. For HO, the world's dominant size, both gauge and scale are the odd amounts (in any units) of 16.5mm and 3.5mm of 1 foot respectively.

However products, parts and plans tailored to these odd amounts are readily available.

The principal scales and gauges used in railroad modelling are listed below. Before going into the mathematics involved and introducing the less frequently used scales, a few figures are given to indicate the general sizes involved. The figures are based on a full-size train length of 820 feet and the 'layout size' indicates the space needed for a double-track circuit. This is formed of two straights equal to that train length joined by two half circles of radius, the minimum suggested for the running of main-line trains.

The Peco Modelrama at Beer, Seaton, Devon, contains a number of layouts on display in a large hall. Various gauges are covered, from N to O, and layouts range from those which use proprietary equipment, and therefore are suitable for beginners, to more advanced types. Each is a model of its kind and shows not only what the different scales look like, but also demonstrates the various ways in which room can be found for them in house or garden.

Below right: A narrow-gauge layout: the Modelrama includes both O-gauge scale on OO-gauge track and OO-gauge scale on N-gauge track.

Below: A proprietary OO-gauge layout in an attic conversion.

TABLE I

Model Railroad Scales

Scale (Fraction)		Train length feet inches		Minimum suggested radius feet inches		Layout size (for double track circuit) feet inches			feet inches	
Full size	(1/1)	820	0	660	0	1360	0	×	2180	0
Z	1:220	3	9	0	7½	1	6	×	5	2
N	1:160	5	2	1	4	3	0	×	8	2
HO	1:87	9	6	2	0	4	6	×	14	0
OO	1:76	10	9	2	3	5	0	×	15	9
S	1:64	12	10	3	0	6	8	×	19	6
O	1:48	17	2	4	6	9	10	×	27	0
O	1:43.5	18	10	4	6	9	11	×	29	9
1	1:32	25	8	6	0	13	3	×	38	11
½-inch	1:24	34	2	12	6	26	8	×	60	10
¾-inch	1:16	51	3	17	6	37	6	×	88	9
1-inch	1:12	68	4	25	0	53	4	×	121	8
1½-inch	1:8	102	6	35	0	75	0	×	177	6
2¼-inch	1:5.3	153	9	50	0	107	6	×	261	3

For those who want to go more deeply into the complexities of model-railroad scales, Table II gives a more exhaustive list of the scales used – the popular sizes are given in heavy type. Against each size is given, first the scale in imperial, metric and fractional measures, then the actual track gauge in both inches and millimeters. This is followed by the full-size equivalent of this track gauge, showing that in some cases there are quite considerable variations from the true Stephenson standard gauge of 4 feet 8½ inches.

The accepted scales and gauges in model railroads range, then, from under ¹⁄₂₀₀ to ½ of full size. If a railroad landscape is what interests you then the ultraminiature N or Z gauge is the answer. If the trains themselves are going to be your pride and joy the universal size of HO/OO is right. O gauge is perhaps the smallest size in which it is reasonable to use the methods and materials of full-size railroads. If you have your line running through real cuttings and embankments dug outdoors in the ground, then 1 gauge is perhaps the smallest size, where the forces of nature do not have things all their own way.

With live steam generated by a real coal fire, then 3½-inch or 5-inch gauge is best, and if you want to haul your friends 7¼-inch is necessary. For hauling the public one needs an even bigger gauge, up to ⅓ or ½ of full size.

Each size has its place but whatever the size, big or small, with the advantage of hindsight it would seem wiser to firmly specify simple scales and let gauges come out at some odd figure, in tenths of millimeters or sixty-fourths of an inch as preferred. After all, the gauge only has to be measured once when you make the template. There is another reason too – the growing number of people who make model railroads built to gauges other than the Stephensonian one. Fantastic railroads abound in the world laid to various broad and narrow gauges from 5 feet 6 inches–1 foot 11½ inches, and for these sizes the choice of a simple dimension as the equivalent of 4 feet 8½ inches does not help at all. Some narrow-gauge model sizes for which commercial material is available are shown in Table III.

TABLE II

Principal Railroad Scales and Equivalents

Name of scale	See chapter	Scale inches to feet	Scale mm to feet	Proportion	Track gauge (for standard-gauge models) inches	mm	Full size equivalent of model track gauge (should be 4' 8½'') feet	inches	Notes	Name of scale
Wakeley		0.0375	0.95	1:320	0.1875	4.76	5	0	Smallest known	Wakeley
Z	4	0.055	1.39	1:220	0.256	6.5	4	8¼	Uncommon as yet	Z
N	**4**	**0.075**	**1.9**	**1:160**	**0.354**	**9**	**4**	**8¾**	**Smallest common size**	**N**
TT	4	0.10	2.54	1:120	0.472	12	4	8¾	Uncommon	TT
TT-3	4	0.118	3	1:102	0.472	12	4	0	Uncommon	TT-3
HO	**5**	**0.138**	**3.5**	**1:87.1**	**0.650**	**16.5**	**4**	**8½**	**World's dominant gauge**	**HO**
HOX (1)	6	0.148	3.75	1:81.3	0.650	16.5	4	4¾	Used secretly	HOX
P4	6	0.157	4	1:76.2	0.741	18.83	4	8½	Known as 'Protofour'	P4
OO	**5**	**0.157**	**4**	**1:76.2**	**0.650**	**16.5**	**4**	**1½**	**Dominant in Britain**	**OO**
EM	6	0.157	4	1:76.2	0.750	19	4	9¼	Rare	EM
S	7	0.1875	4.76	1:64	0.875	22.25	4	8	Uncommon	S
O (2)	8	0.15	6.35	1:48	1.25	32	5	0	USA only and rare	O
O	8	0.265	6.75	1:45.2	1.25	32	4	8¼	Rare and in USA only	O
O (3)	**8**	**0.276**	**7**	**1:43.5**	**1.25**	**32**	**4**	**6½**	**Other than in USA**	**O**
1	9	0.375	9.5	1:32	1.75	45	4	8		1
1	9	0.393	10	1:30.5	1.75	45	4	5½		1
½-inch	9	0.5	12.7	1:24	2.5	63.5	5	0		½-inch
17/32-inch	9	0.531	13.5	1:22.5	2.5	63.5	4	8¼		19/32-inch
¾-inch	10	0.75	19.1	1:16	3.5	89	4	8		¾-inch
1-inch	10	1.0	25.4	1:12	4.75	120	4	9	In USA	1-inch
1 1/16-inch	10	1.0625	27	1:11.3	5.00	127	4	8½	Not in USA	1 1/16-inch
1½-inch	11	1.5	38	1:8	7.25	184	4	10	Not in Western USA	1½-inch
1½-inch	11	1.5	38	1:8	7.50	190	5	0	In Western USA	1½-inch
2-inch	11	2.0	50.8	1:6	9.25	241	4	9		2-inch
2¼-inch	12	2.25	57.2	1:5.333	10.25	260	4	6¾		2¼-inch
3-inch	12	3.0	76	1:4	15	381	5	0		3-inch
4-inch	13	4.0	101.6	1:3	15	381	3	9	Smallest size ever used on a statutory or common-carrier railroad	4-inch
Half size	13	6.0	152	1:2	28½	717	4	8½		Half size
Full size	13	12.0	304.8	1:1	56½	1435	4	8½		Full size

Notes: (1) Certain manufacturers use this scale secretly as a comparable between HO-OO
(2) American O gauge
(3) European O gauge

TABLE III

Some Model Narrow-Gauge Railroad Scales

Name	Scale Name	See chapter	Inches to feet	mm to feet	Proportion	Track gauge Name	inches	mm	Full-size equivalent of model gauge feet	inches	mm	Notes	Name
N6	N	4	0.075	1.0	1:160	Z	0.256	6	3	5	1041	N scale on Z track	N6
TTn3	TT-3	4	0.118	3	1:102	N	0.354	9	3	0⅜	918		TTn3
HOn2	HO	6	0.138	3.5	1:87.1		0.275	7	2	0	610		HOn2
HO9	HO	6	0.138	3.5	1:87.1	N	0.354	9	2	6⅞	784	HO scale on N track	HO9
HOm	HO	6	0.138	3.5	1:87.1	TT		12					HOm
HOn3	HO	6	0.138	3.5	1:87.1		0.413	10.5	3	0	914		HOn3
OO9	OO	6	0.157	4	1:76.2	N	0.354	9	2	3	686	OO scale on N track	OO9
OOn3	OO	6	0.157	4	1:76.2	TT3	0.472	12	3	0	914		OOn3
Sn3	S	7	0.1875	4.76	1:64		0.5625	14.29	3	0	914		Sn3
On2	O	8	0.250	6.35	1:48	½		12.7	2	0	610		On2
On2	O	8	0.275	7	1:43.5			14	2	0	609		On2
On16.5	O	8	0.275	7	1:43.5	OO	0.650	16.05	2	4¼	718	O scale on OO track	On16.5
On3	O	8	0.250	6.35	1:48		¾	19.05	3	0	914		On3
	16mm	9	0.630	16	1:19.1	O	1¼	32	2	0	611		
LGB		9	0.533	13.55	1:22.5	1	11¾	45	3	3⅞	1013	For railroads by LGB	LGB
		11	2.25	57.2	1:5.33		7¼	184	3	2⅝	981	For meter-gauge prototypes	
		11, 12	2.4	60.1	1:5		7¼	184	3	0¼	920	For 3-foot gauge prototypes	
		11	3.6	91	1:3.33		7¼	184	2	0⅛	613	For 600mm & 2-foot gauge prototypes	
		13	6.0	152	1:2		12¼	315	2	0½	330		

Many other combinations of scale and gauge have been developed by individuals from time to time, particularly in the larger sizes. This list is confined to those which are NMRA standards or which have been used by the writer.

There is another reason for there being no point in choosing a round number for the track gauge. This is the fact that the distance between the rails is only one of a number of standard dimensions which need to be fixed in order to give derailment-free running. The most important of these is the distance between the *wheels*, which has to be consistent otherwise trains will never run reliably through points and crossings. The so-called check rails which guide wheels to the correct side of the vees or frogs, which are placed wherever rails cross one another, depend entirely for their functioning on an absolutely consistent dimension between the back of each pair of wheels. Put another way, wheels must suit the trackwork. And vice versa too of course, because the size of the gaps between these check rails and the running rails is yet another place where exact standards need to be defined and adhered to in order to ensure smooth and reliable running.

In the past there was a lack of consistency in this area between the products of one manufacturer and another. Nowadays, thanks to the efforts of the influential National Model Railroad Association (NMRA) in making their standards mandatory in the United States, plus more voluntary co-operation between manufacturers in Europe, there are far fewer sets of wheel and track standards to go with each track gauge. In general it may be taken nowadays that most manufacturers' rolling stock will run on most other manufacturers' track of the same nominal gauge.

For most model railroads electrical standards also need to be fixed. Until very recently 12-volts direct current (DC) was almost universal, combined with two-rail transmission and collection. The German firm of Maerklin (never accustomed to be a follower) still clings to their 16-volt alternating current (AC) system, using rows of connected studs in the center of the track as the current collection medium. Strangely enough, they seem to have held on long enough for AC to come back into fashion, because some of the new digital computerized control systems use 16-volts AC as the base current supplied to the locomotives.

Another matter which may need consideration is compatibility of the couplings between vehicles. In the United States the NMRA requires manufacturers to produce something similar to the knuckle couplers used on North American full-size railroads. In Europe standardization is not yet complete, perhaps because full-size practice in Europe is not a good guide, since the nonautomatic couplings with side buffers used in Europe tend to be unsuitable for model railroads as they give proportionately very sharp curves. The need to change a pair of couplings before bringing a vehicle into service, however, is not usually a very serious matter.

Left: Some firms offer the same models in more than one size. Here are German class 75 2-6-2Ts in N and HO gauge by Merker & Fischer.

Below: The *Flying Scotsman* stands alongside a ⅓ full-size replica in the form of Romney, Hythe & Dymchurch No 3 *Hurricane*.

This vexed question of the sharpest curve that should be used is something that will recur throughout this narrative – and continuously to anyone during the period of building his layout. It is vexed for two reasons, firstly because there is no easy answer and secondly because model railroad curves are normally several times sharper than a true scale one would be. For example on a full-size, main-line, standard-gauge railroad, a curve of half-a-mile radius would be considered severe and would involve a speed restriction. Reduced to HO gauge this half-mile becomes approximately 30-foot radius and so a room 61 feet square would be needed to contain a circle. However, HO trains can go round 3-foot radius curves at full speed. The reason for this is that the dynamics of models are quite different to those of their prototypes and so model trains can negotiate curves sharper than one would ever find in full size, even in sidings. This is all very well, but realism is lost – the beautiful sight of an express train speeding through well-modelled countryside over easy and seductive curves is seldom seen in the model world except (and then only occasionally) in the ultra-miniature sizes.

4 Ultraminiature Railroading

If one's model railroad is laid to one of the ultraminiature sizes there is the most scope for the railroad enthusiast in fashioning the hills and valleys of a railroad country-side. However, the origin and scope of these tiny trains is examined first.

The pioneer of the ultraminiature sizes is considered to be AH Whall, who in 1923 built a complete layout to a scale of 2mm to 1 foot, or $\frac{1}{152}$ of full size, very close to what is now known as N gauge. Of course, every single part was made from scratch with possibly some assistance from the bits and pieces available to the watch-making industry. Whall had quite a few courageous copiers, right down to the time nearly 50 years later when N gauge reached local hobby-shop shelves.

One of the smallest railroads to have been built is one to a gauge of $\frac{3}{16}$ of an inch and in scale $\frac{1}{320}$ of full size. The builder, AR Wakeley, described and illustrated its

one electrically propelled locomotive – a British 0–4–0T dock shunter of Great Western Railway origin – in the *Model Railway News* for June 1936. Rail contacts were made of silver in order to give satisfactory two-rail current collection for a locomotive which turned the scales at a mere quarter of an ounce. Every part, from buffers to armature stampings, was made by the builder. The layout plan adopted – a single unconnected short straight length of track – is far from unknown in real life.

Amateurs having shown the way, professionals in due course began to follow. The road down to the recently introduced Z gauge from HO was long and for some firms painful and took over 50 years. So, having decided to survey the modelling of railroads in ascending order to magnitude, we begin with the last to be introduced. In 1972 the enterprising firm of Maerklin

Right: The beautiful sight of the long trains of a main-line railroad running on easy and seductive curves through pleasant countryside is best reproduced in the ultraminiature sizes. This is the N-gauge Exhibition layout of the Model Railway Club. It was built by a group led by Tim Watson and is based on the practice of the old Midland Railway of England.

Below: A fleet of Peco 'Jubilee' class 4-6-0s are paraded outside the roundhouse of one of the N-gauge layouts at the Peco Modelrama.

introduced to an unbelieving world their Z gauge or 'miniclub' range, $\frac{1}{220}$ of full size. It was 30 percent smaller in dimension than anything offered before.

The advantages of modelling railroads in one of the very small sizes is that more can be fitted into an available space. One could say that the result is like looking down on a landscape from a mountain top rather than, as with the larger sizes, maybe just from the top of a neighboring building.

This is only one of the reasons why the emphasis in Z and N gauges is on the railroad landscape rather than just on the trains. Another is that a smaller variety of rolling stock is available in Z gauge, much less than HO/OO gauge, and it is also relatively more expensive. In addition, because of the minute dimensions, do-it-yourself is more difficult. On the other hand, rolling hills can really roll and one is, as it were, far enough away from, for example, a field of wheat, to notice only the color and not the individual stalks. So a fabric surface, say, is that much better a representation.

The advantages of ultraminiature railroading can be

also looked at the other way round, because of course Z and N sizes can also be used for building a given layout in a very much smaller space – for example a window seat or even a violin case. A layout in N gauge takes only $\frac{1}{4}$ the space that it would in HO and in Z it takes only $\frac{1}{7}$.

Although Z gauge is only offered by that one firm, they are one of the biggest in the business and their range includes six types of steam locomotive, five types of electric locomotive (including a wonderful 'crocodile' articulated) as well as diesels and 15 designs of coach and OO wagons. Curved-track sections come as sharp as $5\frac{3}{4}$ inches in radius (so the idea of a model railroad in a violin case is no absurdity) and there is flexible track for more sweeping installations, as well as points and crossings, including double slip points. Overhead-electrification equipment, signals and every sort of railroad building are also available. Even so, what is available in Z gauge is eclipsed when one thinks of the variety made in N gauge.

In a commercial sense, N-gauge miniature railroads

Below: Proprietary N gauge: one of the N-gauge layouts displayed at the Peco Modelrama at Beer, Devon, England.

began with some push-power model trains made by Lone Star of England from 1950 onward. Although sold as robust toys for a toy-age clientele, they were quite good scale models. The range was later reissued in electric train form but is now no longer on the market. The diesel-outline locomotives had an ingenious and elegantly simple rubber-band drive, but they have been superseded by more conventionally powered models. Although American and British prototypes are produced, the majority of material available is of Continental and in particular German origin and design. What was known as TT gauge, using 3mm to 1 foot scale on 12mm gauge, was offered commercially by Triang of England for several years in the late 1950s and early 1960s. Although the linear scale was only ¾ of OO, the amount of room needed for a given layout was reduced by nearly half. Alas, in respect of the rest of the world the difference between TT and HO (3mm and 3.5mm to 1 foot scale) was really not sufficient for the size to be adopted elsewhere and after a time Triang withdrew it. A faithful group of enthusiasts still carries on (there is

even a TT-gauge society in Britain) either with the original 3mm scale or using a more accurate $\frac{1}{10}$ of an inch to 1 foot scale.

The space an individual has available obviously limits the choice of scale of railroad, but various sites could be exploited. An attic could be used (excellent if the roof, not the floor is, insulated), a cellar (liable to be damp and hence harmful to delicate railroad products) or even a hut in the garden (also liable to be damp unless very well built) but a proper room in the house is certainly best. One reads in many books very fierce advice about railroads but the only kind of instruction that you really need to pay attention to is the correct way of connecting up the electrical connections on your transformer and controller, plus the need for regularity but restraint in lubricating your rolling stock. The rest is much better learned the hard way by making mistakes and correcting them, and by having problems and solving them.

On the other hand, inspiration is a different matter and an author might, and perhaps should, suggest

Below: The possibilities of N gauge: it can even be used in the yard.

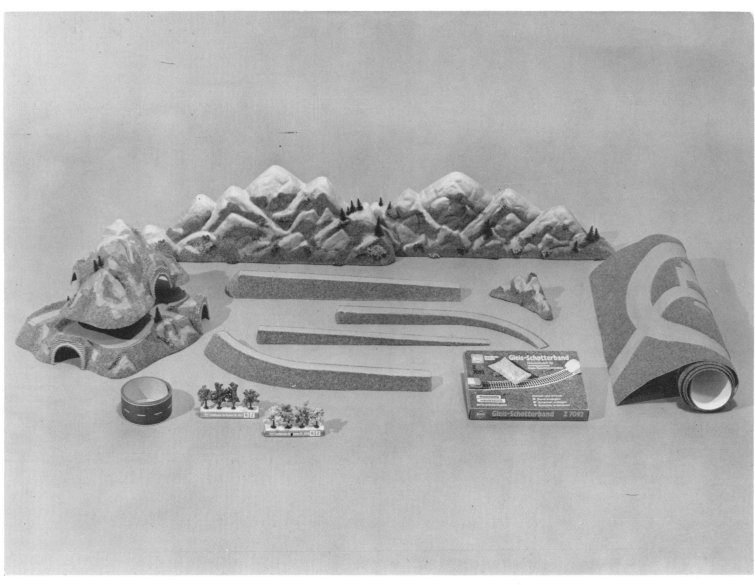

sources of that. The primary source is of course looking to see how a railroad relates to the countryside and of course at the landscape itself. Naturally, if you wish to travel for your inspiration either in time or far away in distance, then books, magazines and pictures must be your guide. A few suggestions are made in the bibliography, and in Chapter 15.

One basic point should be understood before beginning; this is the balance between cuttings and embankments that railroad engineers try and achieve when laying out a railroad grade. Wholly flat landscapes are rather dull and while there are some – much of southern Africa is an example – which are as flat as a table except where relieved by those hills called kopjes, in most of the world railroad grades even out the undulations in the land. The problem for modellers lies in the fact that, while a hill with a railroad cutting in it can be formed on a railroad baseboard easily enough, a declivity crossed by an embankment requires forethought.

One solution is to have a frame rather than a baseboard. A few inches above this are supported shaped pieces of blockboard or plywood to form the subgrades of the line. For the actual supports small vertical pieces of wood are used which, it is suggested, should be screwed rather than nailed for many changes are likely to be made as time goes on. The open baseboard system is a very useful method – one problem solved is that the undersides of hills and dales are accessible. This is helpful in many ways even apart from the possibility of rescuing a train derailed in a tunnel.

Left: This scenery, which is for O gauge, illustrates the principles of construction which apply in all sizes.

Below: Scenery under construction: David Jenkinson, one of Britain's leading experts in this and other aspects of the craft, works on his miniature Garsdale Road layout, based on the legendary Settle & Carlisle line in Northern England.

All sorts of materials can be used to make scenery. A foundation of close mesh-wire netting clad with domestic wall-plaster is one method. Polystyrene, cardboard, card, newspaper, brown paper, cloth, discarded tights, papier-mâché and other discarded trifles can be used. On the other hand specialist scenic modelling materials are also available. Whatever is used the resulting structure can be then sized, painted, anointed with sand, rocks, painted again and then finally demonstrated with pride or pulled down in disgust. The latter hurts less when throwaway materials are used.

Talking of demonstration, artificial scenery – like artificial complexions – should never be shown off in daylight. Instead windows should be blacked out and the layout displayed in stage-type lighting.

A classic and timeless textbook by a master of the craft, the late John Ahern, called *Miniature Landscape Modelling*, first published in 1951, is specially recommended. The book demonstrates its quality by the fact of being still in print (Argus Books, 14 St James Road, Watford, England) 20 years later.

In N gauge at least there is an embarrassing amount of choice in respect of ready-made buildings and it is also fairly easy to make one's own from card or plastic sheet. Many aids in the way of parts and materials are available, as well as realistic trees and shrubs.

As romantic in the world of railroads as The *Super-Chief*, the *Big Boy*, *Royal Scot* or *Flying Scotsman*, are the great bridges. An N-gauge scale model of, say, Brunel's famous Royal Albert Bridge across the River Tamar at Plymouth, England would fit across one 12-foot wall in an average room. Even the curved approaches would fit in admirably – imagine the sight of a double-headed 15-car Cornish Riviera Limited crossing over the two giant spans behind 4-6-0s *Sir Daniel Gooch* and *Isambard Kingdom Brunel!*

Even the highest railroad bridge in the world, the 430-foot high Fades viaduct in France, would not be too tall to be accommodated to N scale between floor and a convenient baseboard height of about 3 feet. The world's longest rail bridge, the 4-mile Huey P Long bridge in New Orleans, USA, would be a bit too much even for Z gauge (at which scale it works out at 65 feet long), but one could certainly get in the bridge with the longest span, and thereby honor a much greater feat of engineering. A Z-scale model of the 1810-foot span steel cantilever bridge of the Canadian National Railways at Quebec would need a 20-foot wall, certainly possible for some railroad enthusiasts. The fact that accurate models of such huge structures would be possible in these ultraminiature sizes illustrates their power and scope better than pages of dialogue.

Left: A vintage scratchbuilt train of clerestory-roofed coaches hauled by a single-wheeler locomotive crossing a viaduct on the four-track main line of Tim Watson's superb Midland Railway layout.

Below right: The end of an N-gauge train: a Union Pacific Railroad caboose by Rivarossi.

Below middle: This lovely decorated Alpine-style inn for N scale is by Pola of West Germany.

Bottom: N-scale down on the farm: note thatched roof, beehives, cottage gardens, cart horses receiving attention to their hoofs, as well as other superb detail by Tim Watson and his team for the Model Railway Club Exhibition layout.

Talking of lesser structures, it is perhaps quite a challenge that those stone-built arched viaducts, the most beautiful of all bridges, are by far the most difficult to make. Even so, the difficulties are minimized in the ultraminiature sizes, where the overall width would be barely more than $3/4$ of an inch for single-track and $1\frac{1}{2}$ inches for double-track structures.

Nothing has so far been said about track and here the reader is referred to the next chapter, where the problems liable to be encountered are dealt with in the context of HO and OO gauges. N and Z gauge have the advantage that, since they developed after HO/OO, many of the lessons learned in the larger size have been applied in the smaller ones.

5   Universal-Scale Models

Unless you are irresistibly drawn to those specialized things which are better done in very small or very big scales, then HO (or OO if British) is for you. The trains are small enough so that an excellent layout can be built in an ordinary room, yet big enough for details on the trains to be seen and appreciated. As this size is by far the most popular, the number of ready-made models in this size is incredible. Steam, diesel and electric are all fully covered. In fact, model manufacturers are beginning to run out of prototypes and Maerklin is currently offering a German 2-6-8-0 Mallet that was only designed and never built, thereby chalking up yet another first for this remarkable firm. Mass production also means that prices are relatively low. Similar availability applies to self-propelled electric, diesel and even steam trains, freight and passenger cars, track, stations, signals, houses, factories, road vehicles and even model people.

To show the upper reaches of the range, one notes such esoteric delights as a working carriage-washing plant (offered by Lima of Italy), heavy rail-mounted 'Big Bertha' style siege guns by Hasegawa of West Germany and Tibetan-style water columns by Mike's Models of Swindon, England. Tibet, of course, has as yet

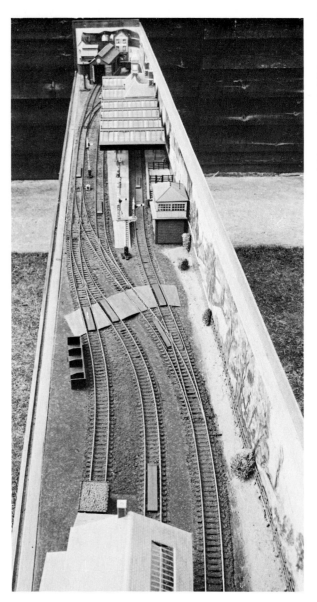

Left: Howley Town, an OO layout on a bookcase, built by Dave Howsam with Peco streamline track.

Right: Southern Railway of England – a model by Arthur Downes in prewar style. A four-car Portsmouth electric express train (miraculously running without the aid of a conductor rail) is at the near platform, the *Bournemouth Belle* with 'Schools' class 4-4-0 Eton to rear. Ex-London & South Western and South Eastern & Chetham 4-4-0s in foreground.

Above: Superdetail extraordinary: a model of a Royal Bavarian State Railways 0-8-8-0T Mallet locomotive, the perfection of which should satisfy the most meticulous enthusiast.

Top: The locomotive that never was: a Borsig articulated Mallet 2-6-8-0 design brought to life in model form by Hamo for DC traction and by Maerklin for AC.

Left: Heavy 'Big Bertha' type artillery piece *Leopold* on two 12-wheel bogie chassis by Hasegawa.

Next page: Henry Orbach's Garve & Ullapool Railway: 'Clan Goods' 4-6-0 No 75 entering Corriehalloch on down 'Sassenach,' with the Garve Valley Tramway in the background.

Bottom: Union Pacific's last steam locomotive, the class FEF 3 4-8-4 No 8444, is here represented by Rivarossi's excellent replica.

Below: Diecast HO-scale model of Richmond, Fredericksburg & Potomac 2-8-4 by Rivarossi.

no railroads, although the Chinese Government has dotted lines on its maps!

Real locomotives do not consist of one-piece castings or moldings inclusive of all details; they are built up from metal sections and sheet, together with individual castings for many parts. This method in any size implies many hours of a craftsman's time and, hence, the deluxe way of acquiring a model locomotive in HO or any other gauge is to go to such a man and give him an order. However this is beyond the means of most people, although they can do it themselves, as described in Chapter 7.

Craftsman-built locomotives did, however, become available in large numbers during the 1950s and 1960s from Japan, where such craftsmen existed in large numbers and where at that time the going rate for skilled work was much lower than that in Western countries. Some production continues, especially in neighboring Korea and Taiwan, but generally the superb brass confections of this period are fast becoming collectors' pieces.

The vast majority of HO/OO locomotives, whether of steam, diesel or electric outline, are electrically driven. For a time Hornby of Britain did in fact offer clockwork models and recently a small firm in England began producing to special order actual working live steam HO/OO models of a fascinating and unusual kind.

As well as ready-made models, manufacturers – mostly of the small backyard kind – offer kits for loco-

motives (and many other accessories) in even greater abundance. More than 120 locomotive prototypes are covered in Great Britain alone, with additions announced every month.

These so-called 'white metal' kits offered by many small firms, particularly in Britain, have the advantage that simple metal patterns are all that is required as a preliminary to producing the parts. The investment is very low compared with the cost of the equipment needed for large-scale production and this facilitates the making of kits to represent many rare delights of the full-size railroad world.

Although the actual production process is much more expensive, the same advantage applies over the small investment needed to produce brass locomotive and car details by the so-called 'lost wax' or 'investment casting' process. Such parts are certainly far superior to their white metal counterparts and are used for the making of the lovely brass locomotives described above, as well as for scratchbuilding. The North American market is particularly well supplied with these beautifully produced models.

It is fair to say that most of the model-railroad layouts of the world are in HO/OO, and this applies equally to the most advanced and greatest of them as to beginners' first layouts on the floor or table top. The only fault with this universal size is that found in all compromises, that is, if one wants to model the relationship of railroads with the countryside, then HO/OO is just

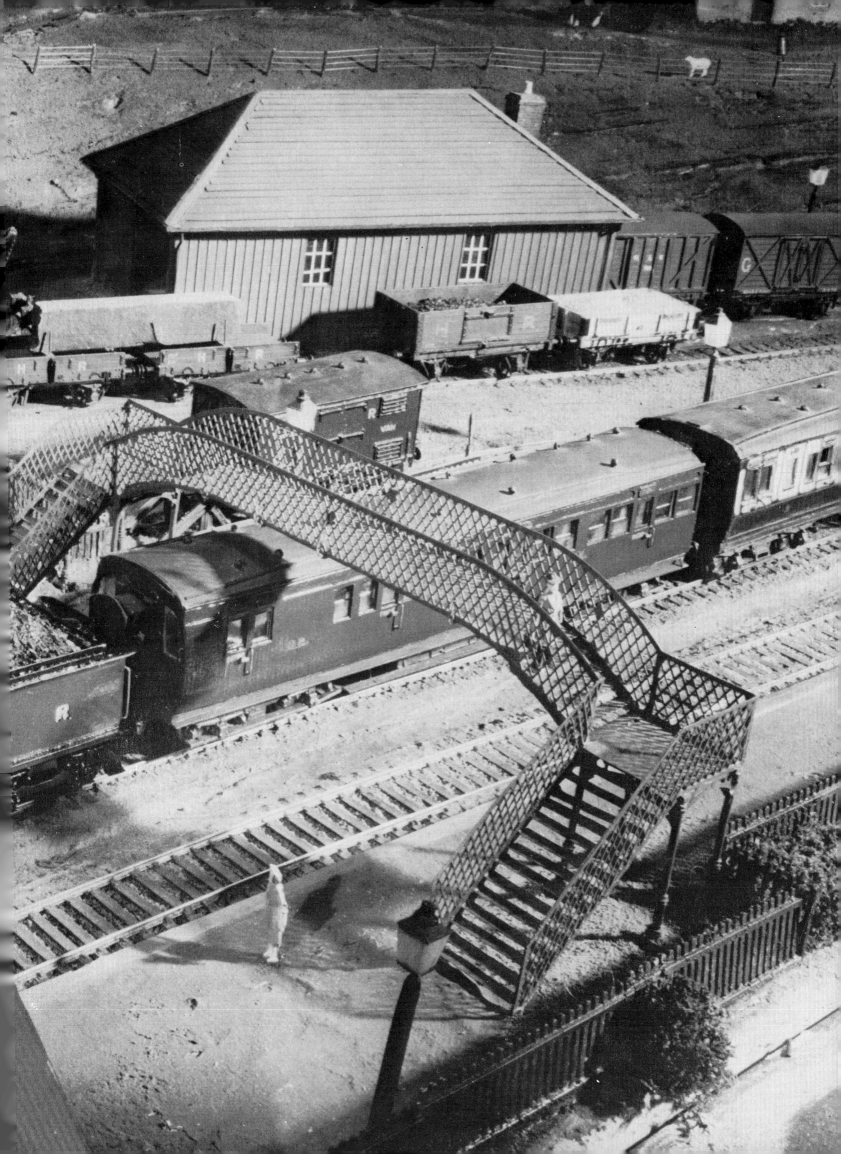

a trifle large, while for very exact modelling of actual locomotives and cars, then the scale is rather too small. However, if one wants to do a bit of both, then HO/OO is the size to use.

The typical beginner enters the game in one of two ways. He may either be influenced by the layout of a friend or neighbor, or he will buy a train set at his local dealer or model shop. Either way he is liable to come home with an HO or OO electric train, a transformer and controller, a circle or oval of track and one or two turnouts to make into sidings. Soon enough this train is chasing its tail round the circle, laid out either on a table or on the floor and, of course, put away afterward.

While it is often said that this arrangement is totally unrailroadlike, there is a prototype for everything and in this case it is a nearly circular line laid out to serve, with passenger and freight trains, a big shell-filling factory at Thorp Arch, Yorkshire, England. Each part of the factory was widely separated from the others (for

reasons that no one really liked to dwell upon) and so the arrangement was a convenient one. Like a man's first model railroad this particular train set has also now been put away!

It must be said that, instead of a continuous circuit, it is better to run as real railroads usually do, from one place to another. The snag is that, even if you accept a railroad having stations only a mile apart, when reduced to HO or OO scale this mile becomes a 60-foot long trunk route. Railroads have been likened to a stage show and it is therefore appropriate to have an off-stage section of the system. This is disrespectfully known as a 'fiddle yard' and is an adjunct of most realistically operated railroad systems. Certainly it is essential if one aims at the highest form of railroad modelling – the re-creation of some actual railroad station in miniature as a true historical or contemporary representation.

However one should certainly not disdain layouts which are quickly put down and taken up again, even

Left: Old Timer: the first train to run in Germany, hauled by the *Adler* ('Eagle') loco, by Trix of Nuremberg in HO gauge.

Right: *County Kilkenny* by Mr A J East of Harrogate, England. Chassis, loco body and tender awaiting detailing (below), and the locomotive complete (above). This locomotive is scratchbuilt.

Below left: A North Eastern Railway 4-4-0 leaves Altbeg Station on PD Hancock's 4mm scale model railroad.

BANGOR and MACHIAS RAILROAD

Hereby Issues This PASS

To _____

Date of Issue _____

Subject to Conditions on back.

BANGOR & MACHIAS · RAILROAD · SERVES EASTERN MAINE

N° 255

Paul Huntington, Pres.

CONDITIONS

1. This pass good on all trains of the BANGOR AND MACHIAS RAILROAD except for trains #1 and #2, The Maritime Limited.
2. Good also on trains of subsidiary BANGOR NORTHERN (narrow gauge line)
3. This railroad not to be referred to by terms "cute" or a "train set".
4. Children under 6 must be kept on a leash.
5. Suggestions for improvements will be cheerfully ignored.
6. In case of derailment leave train and run forward to warn engineer.
7. Passengers will please refrain while the train is in the station.

General Offices: 176 SOUTH STREET   RANDOLPH, MASS.

TRAVEL BY TRAIN - - - - SHIP BY RAIL

Left: Travel on the Bangor & Machias is facilitated by a pass issued by the President.

Below: The same week that the United States entered World War II, the New York Central Railroad inaugurated the streamlined Empire State Express service from New York to Detroit via Canada. A model of this train runs on South Oakland County Model Railroad Club, Birmingham, Michigan, USA.

Right: Scotland in the USA: 'Barney' 0-6-0 No 134 about to shunt Corriehalloch yard 'Yankee' tank 102 waiting in the bay with a horsebox, on Henry Orbach's Highland Railway model.

Previous page: Peco Modelrama: a heavy influx of extra motive power swamps the tiny Great Western-style locomotive-servicing facility on the Candleford Mill layout.

Top: Continental luxury in HO gauge: Rivarossi's blue and gold dining car of the Compagnie Internationale des Wagons Lits.

Left: Mass-produced locomotive improved by specialist parts: this is an East German class 01.5 4-6-2 by Piko, but with wheels, valancing and other detail by Gerard. Note such detail as the difference between the size of the balance weights on the driving and on the coupled wheels.

Below: A lady's layout: Vivien Thompson's London Brighton & South Coast Railway's goods depot.

Above: Ann Arbor as represented on the layout of the South Oakland County Model Railroad Club. This view shows the main lifting bridge and the junction with an intercity electric line.

Next page: People watching a train depart from Candleford Mill Station.

though formed from standard proprietary track sections, turnouts and so on, because this is the best way to learn the principles and problems involved. One soon finds out, for example, why full-size railroads prefer to connect sidings to the main line in such a way that, in the normal direction of running, a train has to be backed in – in railroad parlance, this means a trailing point – otherwise, a wrongly set switch leads to something fairly spectacular in the way of high-speed railroad wrecks rather than a few wheels off the line. Of course, one should also know things like the fact that on double lines British, French, Swiss, Italian and Japanese trains keep to the left, while German and North American ones keep to the right.

Problems peculiar to model railroads because they are associated with the two-rail system of electrification are also liable to come to light. For example, on a reverse or return loop very peculiar things happen because one has effectively connected each running rail to its opposite number. In fact, a special switch and insulated track section is needed. There is also the subtle distinction between a turnout with a live frog and one with an insulated frog. The former is best used for sidings as they only leave connected the line for which the points are set while the latter – more appropriate in a junction – keeps continuity through both lines of the turnout regardless of the setting of the points. Some manufacturers provide both types as complementary alternatives, thereby giving the correct answer to a controversy which has plagued the two-rail world for decades.

Other things that it is best for the beginner to learn the hard way include the importance of a perfectly smooth connection at rail joints, the need to avoid any twist or wind in the track and that superelevation or cant on sharp curves is better avoided on model railroads.

While a temporary layout implies track sections of fixed length and curvature, once a permanent layout is achieved then it is possible to use what is called flexible track. Metal rails are supplied fixed into fastenings of a plastic molding which cleverly represents a row of railroad sleepers. This molding is not rigid and the resulting assembly can be bent into curves and S-bends before being fixed to the baseboard. This is usually done with small pins or screws for which holes in the plastic are provided. Care must be taken that the flexible track is not curved even momentarily into bends that trains cannot negotiate. A fixed curve section of line can be used as a 'no-go' gauge. Timber, concrete and narrow-gauge types of track are provided and material is available for N and O gauge as well as HO/OO. Note that because the outer rail of a curve has to be longer than the inner one, rail ends of flexible-track lengths need trimming with a fine-toothed metal saw before they can be joined together.

Traditional British track was laid with 60-foot long rails of which the scale equivalent is 10 inches. In fact, flexible track, coming as it does in yard or meter lengths is much more akin in this respect to the continuous welded rail of today. If you want the true 'clickety-click' of steam-age travel it is necessary to notch the running surface of each rail four times in each yard length. For historical models which go back to the 45-foot or even 30-foot track used before World War I, distance between notches should be proportionately reduced. American steam-age railroading, on the other hand, sounded the tune of the staggered joints of 39-foot rails, so a notch on alternate sides at $2\frac{1}{2}$-inch intervals would be in order. In the United States steam-age track has long survived the end of the iron horse itself.

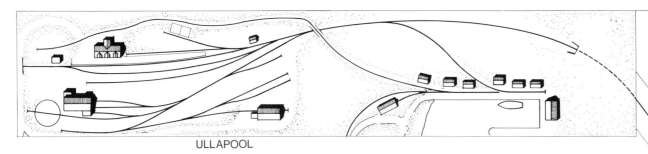

ULLAPOOL

0 1 2 3 4 5 6 7 8
FEET

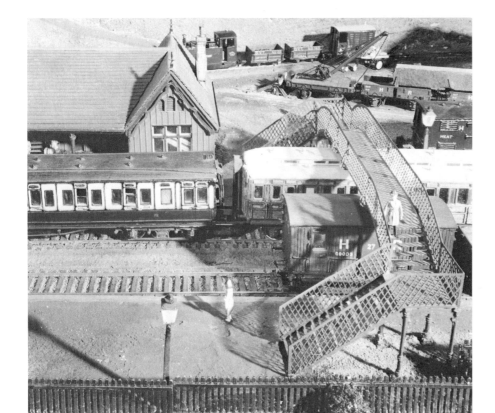

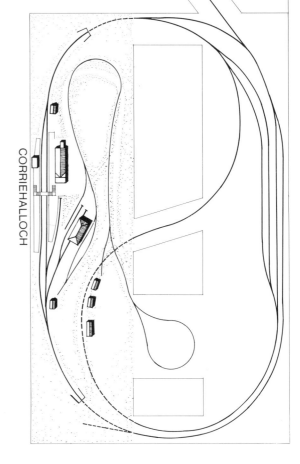

CORRIEHALLOCH

Above: The plan of Henry Orbach's Garve and Ullapool Railway in Birmingham, Michigan.

Left: HR 0-4-4T No 25 'Strathpeffer' is about to leave Ullapool on the 0625 train to Garve and Dingwall. 'Barney' 0-6-0 No 134 is shunting, and 'Yankee' 0-4-0T 102 and 'Ben Alder' 4-4-0 No 2 is on shed.

Above left: A London & North Western double-ended brake slip coach and East Coast Joint Stock composite at Corriehalloch.

There is a problem here in that OO scale British permanent way (which uses 10-inch by 5-inch sleepers spaced at 30-inch intervals) should have 3.3mm by 4.6mm sleepers spaced at 10mm intervals, while its HO American counterpart (with 7-inch by 7-inch sleepers spaced at 22-inch intervals) needs 2mm by 2mm sleepers spaced at 6.3mm. In this imperfect world the same molding has to serve for both, as well as for European Continental practice, which lies between the two. However only a very few permanent way pedants notice such things.

Most prototype railroads have signalling systems and here again there is a distinction between the old semaphore signals (some of which still exist) and colored light signals of modern times (but which were not unknown 50 years and more ago). Proprietary HO/OO signals covering both the distinctive mechanical and electrical signalling, of most varieties, are available.

However, full signalling of any kind is very complex not only to install but also to maintain and operate. If you must have it, the only hope is to make a specialist signalling layout, perhaps best done like live steam in a larger gauge. In HO/OO where the idea is usually to give a general picture of railroading, it is more prudent to suggest a signalling system with a few conspicuous signals arranged to be worked by the trains instead of vice versa.

The buildings and structures of an HO/OO gauge model railroad offer tremendous scope for an imaginative approach. Of course, there is an immense range available – from fully finished and detailed models to molding sets which enable something approaching real building materials to be used in do-it-yourself projects. That legendary Scottish clergyman, Edward Beal, long ago showed the way when he finished off a row of houses with a model of one under construction. Of course, most model-rail enthusiasts naturally put most effort into the many buildings connected with the railroad, such as stations, freight depots, locomotive sheds and signal boxes.

Similarly, not to be forgotten are all the finishing touches needed to complete the scenic picture, such as lamp posts, platform seats, fencing, road vehicles and, of course, people themselves, for whose transportation the railroad has been built.

Below: Candleford people awaiting the train on Candleford Mill Station.

Above: Bangor Roundhouse: power-operated turntable. The details were taken from an actual installation of the Boston & Maine.

Right: A refrigerator car – 'reefer' for short – on Irv Schultz' St Clair Northern Railroad.

Far right: The modern railroad – David Bowes' diesel- and electric-powered layout.

71

6 Offshoots and Derivatives

It is not surprising that a size of model train as popular as HO/OO should have many offshoots and derivatives. Firstly, there are those in Britain who try and correct the anomaly implicit in using 16.5mm gauge with 4mm scale for models of standard gauge trains. This is done either by using a nearly correct gauge of 18mm – in Britain this size goes under the name of EM – or by adopting an exactly-to-scale gauge of 18.83mm, with all the ancillary wheel and track standards also exactly to scale and to very fine limits. The name of this arrangement is 'Protofour' (P4) and it is definitely not for beginners. For EM gauge, on the other hand, ready-made wheels can be used and various small firms offer a conversion service.

In Protofour there is no question of running down to see one's local dealer and coming back with a packet of yard lengths of flexible track ready to fix down. Both because of the special gauge and because of other shortcomings of ready-to-wear permanent way – much too close sleeper spacing is usual – it is necessary to fix down one hundred or more individual sleepers for each length and then spike the rails to them in chairs or baseplates as appropriate. So tracklaying in Protofour is like doing it in the larger sizes, up to and including 12 inches to 1 foot scale, but with the difference that the precision needed in the small size is so much greater. This applies particularly to points and crossings as well as wheel dimensions.

For example, a full-size wheel is 5¾ inches thick; in OO (1:76 scale) this becomes 1.92mm. Well and good, but the normal thickness of wheels on good quality HO/OO model trains as bought off-the-shelf is 3mm, nearly twice as much. These 'steam-roller' wheels cater for running over the wide oblique gaps which occur in the running surfaces of the rails at crossings. The width of these gaps is, in the model world, standardized at about twice the scale amount, that is 1.34mm instead of 0.6mm.

A further complication arises over the wheels in this very precise type of model railroading. On a model locomotive, wheels are perhaps the most difficult items to make oneself. Since they also include the largest

Above: Peter Denny's famous Buckingham Central in EM gauge, that is, 4mm to 1 foot scale running on 18mm gauge. The system brings back to life the old Great Central Railway at the turn of the century, when the line from Nottingham to London (Marylebone) was opened.

Left: Grandborough Junction on Peter Denny's superb EM-gauge layout.

Right: A Great Western freight train entering the tunnel on the Pendon Museum layout.

Left: Steam-driven 2-8-0T Great Western tank locomotive designed by Professor Sherwood of Sydney, Australia.

Below right: A superb HOn3 brass model of a Denver & Rio Grande Western class K-36, 2-8-2. It runs on 10.5mm track.

Below: Class C59: the definitive and last Japanese Pacific-type passenger engine, used for main-line express trains.

measure of repetition, they therefore have always been among the first items to be offered commercially in a new scale. However, in very precise work, small differences between wheels of the same nominal size, for example, the number of spokes or whether the crankpin boss is in line with one of them or in between two adjacent ones, must be considered. So the measure of repetition and hence the chances of a commercial product being available for the model being made, are reduced. Studiolith of Rofford, Little Milton, Oxford, offer materials and parts for P4.

One strange quirk of the model-train world is the existence of a clandestine scale on the part of a few European manufacturers. If a firm offers both Continental and British equipment in the same range, the Continental trains are naturally made to the 3.5mm to 1 foot scale, the British ones then present a problem. If they are made to the British 4mm scale, the height (13 feet at 4mm scale equals 52mm) exceeds that (14 feet 6 inches at 3.5mm scale equals 51mm) of a Continental train; if made to 3.5mm scale, the model looks absurd among British-made 4mm ones. Moreover, being so small, standard motors will probably not fit. The equally unsatisfactory course of action adopted by one or two nameless manufacturers is to compromise with a discreetly unannounced 3.75mm scale.

One of the best as well as one of the biggest ranges of HO commercial model railroads is also quite non-standard. It should be no surprise that the culprit is our old friend Maerklin, who has been making the size for nearly 50 years, it now being their principal range. The incompatibility with standard methods occurs not only in one but in two ways, both quite basic ones.

The first (which has already been mentioned) is that the current supply to the trains is alternating not direct current. Now AC motors, unlike permanent-magnet DC ones cannot be reversed by the simple process of reversing the current at the controller. It is necessary instead to have a small electromechanical relay on the locomotive which responds to a slight overvoltage, produced by pressing a button on the controller. The locomotive relay responds by taking, in sequence, the positions forward, stop, reverse, stop, forward and so on, each time the button is pressed. Fifty years of development has made the system extremely reliable, although it sounds complicated. The idea of a relay on the locomotive for control purposes is coming into fashion again owing to the numerous silicon-chip developments. It is understood that a substitute electronic relay for the Maerklin system will soon be available.

The second incompatibility is in the method of conveying traction current to the trains. Instead of using the two running rails as separate conductors in the usual way, Maerklin use *both* running rails as one conductor and a row of studs as the other. 'Skate' collectors on the locomotives are always in contact with

one or more studs. When they began in HO in the 1930s the then usual separate central conductor rail was used. This was criticized on the grounds of realism and after the war this unobtrusive stud-contact system was introduced.

A live conductor separate from the running rails avoids some oddball electrical problems with certain types of layout and also makes such things as automatic signalling more straightforward. It is also possible that, given Maerklin's dominant position, they take advantage of the fact that patrons might be discouraged from going elsewhere because other firms' trains are incompatible.

This is not entirely valid because much of the huge range of Maerklin motive power – 40 separate items not counting color variations – is also available as two-rail DC under the trade name *Hamo*. One can also fairly easily convert standard two-rail items to stud-contact, but not so easily to AC. It is also fairly significant that Maerklin's more recently introduced ranges are two-rail. Their Z gauge has two-rail DC, while in 1 gauge the option of DC or AC is offered. Incidentally, although it is not mentioned in the instruction book, Maerklin AC trains will run well on DC, although reversing needs to be done manually, with the lever provided. Lilliput offer AC as an option for their superb HO range.

Specialties of the Maerklin HO range also include flexible stud-contact track, a locomotive or vehicle traverser as well as turntables and the most comprehensive collection of mechanical and electric signals ever offered – 15 different types of signal are available.

Mr David Taylor of Steamcraft, Southport, Lancashire, England, has recently announced a range of gas-fired live-steam locomotives to British OO scale and some North American items in HO. Some simplification is necessary in this size because nature (in the live-steam sense) cannot be scaled down. For example, Steamcraft locomotives have only a single cylinder, but geared down 2:1 to give the correct four beats to each turn of the driving wheels. Since they are cast in solid brass to exact scale appearance, the models are both robust and good-looking. They are intended to operate on the same layout as normal electric model trains. Their electrical control has yet to be perfected, but this cannot be far away.

As well as unusual motive power, unusual railroads and other related means of guided land transport are also catered for. The German firm of Fleischmann also offer, as a supplement to their comprehensive but otherwise more orthodox HO range, the unusual feature of a rack-and-pinion railroad system. This is also available in N gauge. Orthodox railroads, big or small, are in general limited to gradients less than 1 in 25, but cogwheel assistance enables the gradient to be increased to 1 in 3. You can reach a railroad baseboard from the floor in 9 feet using the standard Fleischmann track to which their flexible rack section has been

Above: The model of a Brunel timber viaduct at the Pendon Museum. A milk, parcels and mail train is crossing.

Above right: Maerklin: Royal Bavarian Railways 4-6-2 for stud-contact operation. Fitted with working headlights, automatic uncoupling and smoke unit.

Right: Denver & Rio Grande Western 2-8-0 and 2-8-2 locomotives on the narrow-gauge section of the South Oakland County Model Railroad Club layout, Birmingham, Michigan.

Left: Linslade Station on Peter Denny's 4mm scale Great Central model railroad.

Above and below: Bucks Harbor station on Paul Huntington's HOn3 narrow-gauge line.

attached. As yet, however, their rack locomotives are merely ordinary adhesion ones modified. However, one does note one or two specialist suppliers, such as Gerard of Switzerland, who offer 'batch-produced' rather than mass-produced scale cog-railway items at a correspondingly higher price. A funicular railway is offered by Brawa of West Germany. Akin to this but in fact not true railways are the cable-car and ski-lift systems offered by the same firm.

The richest HO and OO derivatives are the models of narrow-gauge trains made to these scales but to lesser gauges. The narrow gauge came into being as a way of making railroads cheaply, but the slow speeds on these lines made them exceptionally vulnerable to road competition, while their old and unusual equipment gave them exceptional and lasting charm.

It must be said at the outset that, in contrast to the real world, narrow-gauge model railroads tend to be more, not less, expensive than full-size ones, mainly because the numbers made are smaller. The arrival of N gauge gave a boost to the narrow-gaugers, making chassis available to them at mass-production prices. The distance (9mm) between N-gauge rails works out to HO scale as the equivalent 2 feet 7 inches; for OO scale the equivalent is 2 feet 3 inches.

Of course, narrow-gauge proper begins with the famous 'Cape Gauge' of 3 feet 6 inches, common all over Africa and the Far East. Many Cape Gauge systems, notably those of South Africa and Japan, are built to the heaviest main-line standards. Of 3-foot 6-inch gauge countries only Japan mass produces model railroads. Although they are not seriously marketed in Europe or the United States, samples which have been examined indicate that something close to the British 4mm scale is used by such firms as Katsumi. In conjunction with 16.5mm gauge, this scale gives proportions which are close enough for all but the most critical eyes. Outside Japan, the range of 'Cape Gauge' model railroading is poor indeed, although Lima of Italy do a South African electric suburban train.

Meter-gauge railroads occur very frequently both in Europe and elsewhere. Many of them are also fairly solid prosperous main-line affairs, but others are quaint and local. The size is catered for surprisingly little by manufacturers, though one notes with approval the West German firm of Bemo recently offering 'HOm' 12mm gauge models of electric trains which run on the Rhaetian Railway meter-gauge network in Southeastern Switzerland. Zeuke of East Germany also offer this size.

Left: Irish broad gauge. Mr R Chown's Castle Rackrent, Moygraney & Pacific Railway; it is 4mm scale on 21mm gauge, correct for the Irish standard of 5 feet 3 inches.

Below left: Bucks Harbor locomotive depot, with 2-8-0 No 9.

Right: An HO scale on 9mm-gauge 0-10-0 modelled on an East German prototype, by Merker and Fischer.

Batch production rather than mass production has made it reasonably easy to provide modellers with replicas of the hardware than ran on the legendary American 3-foot gauge railroads that were built in the mountainous states of Colorado, New Mexico and elsewhere. From Japan came brass models of the locomotives and even metal replicas of wooden passenger cars. Incidentally, a few years later, the Denver & Rio Grande Western RR did just that in full size, in order to provide passenger accommodation for their tourist traffic explosion. Flexible track to a true 10.5mm gauge is available, plus kits for every imaginable type of car, facility and building.

These so-called tiny engines of the United States narrow gauge were in fact as big and powerful as anything that ran in Britain on the standard gauge during the steam era. For the true flavor of such things it is necessary to go one stage slimmer in respect of gauge and, as already mentioned, there was a convenient stopping point at 9mm, the dimension which was coming into use under the name N gauge. As soon as N-gauge mechanisms and chassis became available white-metal cast kits also became available to fit new narrow-gauge bodies to them. The available range covers most reasonably well-known prototypes of a not very wide field. This combination of scale and gauge is called either HOe or 009 according to whether the scale is HO or OO respectively. HOn $2\frac{1}{2}$ is the American term.

The demand for narrow-gauge railroads of local interest is great enough in Europe to support mass production, principally supplied by the Austrian firm of Lilliput. Happily there was a big element of standardization among the various Austrian narrow-gauge lines, both private and public, which enables the same old-timer 0-6-2T, for example, to be offered as for the Salzkammergutlokalbahn, the Zillertalbahn and the Styrian Local Government Railway, as well as the Austrian Federal Railways themselves. The 9mm gauge is almost exactly to scale for these lines, which in the original have, rather surprisingly, a gauge of $2\frac{1}{2}$ feet. This betrays an origin in material via Austrian military railroads acquired cheap from a contractor engaged on the construction of the Suez Canal – thereby illustrating the point that no model railroad story can be as fantastic as those relating to real railroads. Firms such as Peco of Sidmouth, England, offer 9mm flexible track with typically random narrow-gauge sleepers.

Some of the loveliest of the narrow-gauge lines were laid to an even narrower gauge, one where the metric dimension of 600mm almost coincides with 2 feet. In fact, Z gauge (6mm) would be fairly close to being correct for HO scale for 2-foot gauge but unfortunately quite apart from the fact that Z gauge is still very new, there is the problem that most 2-foot gauge locomotives have what are called outside frames. In this arrangement, which also applies to locomotives in gauges of up to 3 feet, the wheels are inside the frames, and the motion drives on separate cranks outside them. Accordingly, the use of a chassis from a smaller scale is not really satisfactory, while the fine and detailed work necessary to build one's own is beyond the skill of most people.

As indicated in the table in Chapter 3, the NMRA do offer standards for HOn2 models, with a gauge of 0.138 inches (7mm), and certain parts are available. However, except for an occasional brass handmade model, nothing in the way of ready-to-run material is offered.

Going from one extreme to the other, it is notable that railroads which use a broader gauge than 4 feet $8\frac{1}{2}$ inches are in their turn ignored by most modellers. Even those few broad-gauge countries which make model railroads ignore the scale effect of the wider spacing of their full-size metals. Electrotren of Spain, for example, offer excellent HO scale models of Spanish as well as other trains, but use the standard gauge of 16.5mm instead of the scale equivalent of the Spanish 5 feet 6 inches, which would be 19.25mm.

In OO scale, a few Irish items for 21mm gauge (the equivalent of 5 feet 3 inches at 4mm to 1 foot) are offered by the Model Wagon Company of West Kilbride, Scotland. Perhaps most romantic of all, and nowadays hardly less nostalgic than steam traction itself, is the wonderful world of real broad gauge, Isambard Kingdom Brunel's 7 feet $\frac{1}{4}$ inch Great Western Railway. This was a world in which locomotives were never numbered, but given names like *Iron Duke*, *Hirondelle* or *Lord of the Isles*, and in which a locomotive superintendent could personally drive his sovereign's consort, Prince Albert, home from Bristol after the launching of the greatest steamship then afloat. The time of 2 hours 4 minutes for an 118-mile intercity journey was one which would be out of reach for many railroads today, let alone those of 1843, when this amazing run took place. A kit for the type of locomotive (Daniel Gooch's 'Fire Fly' class 2-2-2) which performed this feat, plus cars for the train, can still be obtained from Model Railway Services Ltd, Manchester. If originality in model railroading appeals to you, look no further!

7 Scratchbuilding and S Gauge

When the step from one gauge to the next is double, as is the case when moving from HO ('Half-Ought') to O, there seems to be the need to insert an intermediate size, which is how S gauge arose. However it is a very bold modeller who sets out to explore the delights of S gauge, for he enters what is still pioneer country. He does begin with one advantage, however, because $\frac{3}{16}$ of an inch to 1 foot scale on $\frac{7}{8}$-inch gauge is one of those rare sizes where 'nice' dimensions give correct scale proportions – mainly because 7 is a factor of both the model gauge and the full-size standard one of almost 56 inches.

The size chosen was in fact not quite halfway, but biased toward the smaller size and this has rather discouraged any development of S gauge in Britain. The difference between OO ($\frac{1}{76}$ of full size) and S ($\frac{1}{64}$ of full size) is a little small for it to be really worthwhile to adopt a new scale. Even so a few independently minded Englishmen (Alan Cruickshank, who writes in the magazine *Model Railways* on scratchbuilding locomotives, is one) do model in this size.

In the United States S gauge has a certain following. For one thing $\frac{1}{64}$ scale is much further from $\frac{1}{87}$ (HO) than $\frac{1}{76}$ (OO) and for another a very famous and superior line of toy trains was once offered in this convenient S-gauge size. These were the Gilbert Corporation's American Flyer Trains. The rolling stock was copied fairly exactly from some handsome and unusual new passenger cars introduced by the New York, New Haven & Hartford RR in 1927. In fact, externally they followed European rather than American style. Inevitably the full-size trains got dubbed American Flyer and it happened that the combination of great comfort, coupled with the fact of their looking like familiar toy trains, caught the public's imagination. Other Eastern roads such as the Boston & Maine ordered similar ones – a surprising interaction between big trains and little ones.

It's popularity in the United States has led to some modest backing from the smaller firms in the trade. There is even a magazine called the *S-Gaugian* (PO Box 66, Tolono, Illinois 61880) specializing in this rare size. Material for 3-foot gauge prototypes is also offered in $\frac{9}{16}$-inch gauge under the title Sn3. An attractive scale would be a hypothetical Sn3½, which would mean the use of 16.5mm-gauge mechanisms and track together with some superb possibilities among the Cape Gauge railroads of the world.

However, such short cuts would be entirely foreign to the mind of the true S-gauge enthusiast who chose S

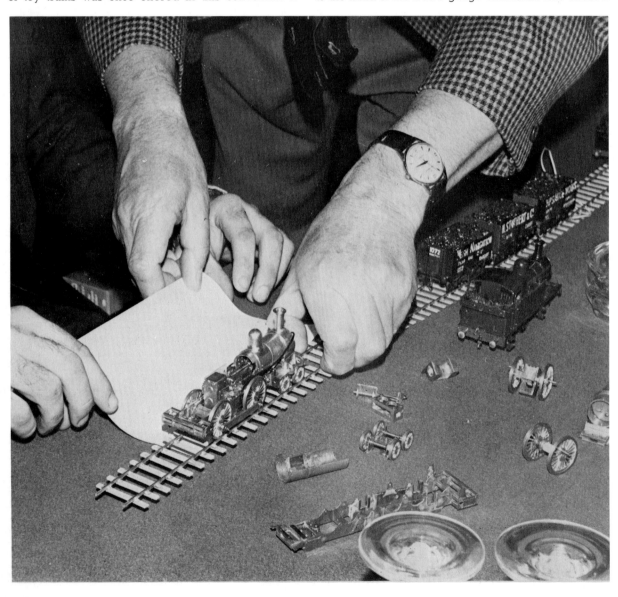

Left: S gauge under construction: members of the S-gauge Society of Britain engaged on model railroad making in this unusual size.

Above right: A scratchbuilt 2-8-0 from the collection of EJ Gulash of Dearborn, Michigan.

Right: Cab detail on hand-built models: left to right, London, Midland & Scottish *Compound* 4-4-0, *Royal Scot* 4-6-0 and *Princess Royal* 4-6-2.

gauge not in spite of but because the road to success in this size is so long and hard. The reward, of course, is freedom from the shackles of having to buy exactly what manufacturers think you ought to – in a phrase, in S gauge there is no distraction from modelling the unmodelled. Also of course, there is the satisfaction that comes from an achievement that has absolutely no ambiguity about it, for make no mistake, the construction of even a reasonably nice scratchbuilt model is a considerable feat.

Of course, models can be and are built from scratch in any size. The principal merits and drawbacks of so doing hardly differ. As regards the widening of scope that results, one finds that so far as many countries are concerned, it is difficult to think of any type of locomotive not yet modelled. This certainly applies to Britain and to some extent also to both Europe and to the United States. However, elsewhere, why not consider such subjects as those legendary *Andes* 2-8-0s, in bright green livery with lama's head emblem? A few of the 16 zigzags which take the Central of Peru Railway up to its 15,640-foot summit might take an S-gauge line with

ones, are appreciated enough to be preserved in museums and in any case often lie around in sidings and dumps long after their service days are over, hence they are there to be looked over.

Rolling stock is less likely to be appreciated enough for long-term survival but even then items stay around for a surprising length of time. The writer recalls crawling under some old clerestory-roofed carriages in sidings near Oxford to find out whether the central compartment had originally been two extra lavatories. These had been necessary because in the early days of corridor trains in Britain, toilets were segregated not only by class but by sex. Yes, the two round holes were there, and in the end a correct model was achieved of this car in its original condition. Incidentally, the term scratchbuilding, as defined by the National Model Railroad Association does not mean that you have to dig your own metal ores from the ground. A little assistance from miners, metal refiners and woodcutters is allowed, through such matters as the purchase of metal, wood and plastic sheets and sections. The following finished parts are also permitted: motor, gears, wheels, coup-

Left: Scratchbuilt and clockwork: a delightful 0-4-4T from the old Great Southern & Western Railway of Ireland by Drew Donaldson of Dublin.

Andes locomotives up from a basement (with port facilities) to a terminus in an attic. Or try the only steam locomotives still in production in the world today, the Chinese 'March Forward' class 2-10-2. Again, there are sets of working drawings and works photographs for all the fabulous Beyer-Garratt articulated locomotives lying in the basement of the North West Museum of Science and Industry in Manchester, England, just waiting for modellers to demand copies.

So, coming down to earth after these flights of fancy, a point is reached which needs making. When building from scratch where does one go for information? Many of the helping hands are described in Chapter 15 but it is very hard to beat, or indeed do without, personally running a rule, as well as pointing a camera in close-up, all over the locomotive or other item involved. One reason is that different locomotives of a class are individuals and have a way of differing significantly from one another and from the works drawings, so one wants to know the idiosyncrasies of the actual one intended to be modelled. Naturally, if you were not the sort of person who would concern himself with such pedantic detail, then you would not be undertaking scratchbuilding, or be involved in S gauge at all. Happily, many obsolete locomotives, particularly steam

lers, bogies or trucks (if correct pattern), marker lights and bulbs, bells and brake fittings.

The techniques of scratchbuilding are not far removed from those of the workshops in which the original was made. Perhaps brass or nickel silver is substituted for steel, and soldering for welding, but many of the problems remain similar. The necessity for jigs is one, as is the need for absolute squareness, flatness and perpendicularity. The danger of distortion after heat is applied in the joining-up process is particularly worrying to both full-size and model foremen and so on. A classic textbook on the subject is John Ahern's book on locomotive construction, published in 1938 but still available. Since then many advances have been made, but there is little change in the basic principles involved.

One very tedious aspect of the work is the need to make batches of certain components. While a locomotive will have only one chimney, it may have six, eight or more tender axle boxes. A carriage may have a dozen roof vents, or a gantry signal five or six arms, lamps and finials. Tedious repetition can be avoided since, having made one part as a pattern, it can easily be duplicated in brass by the lost-wax process or in white metal by a related casting system.

Above: Hand built and handsome: a Great Central (but lettered for London & North Eastern) Class A5 4-6-2T.

Below: Perfection in handmade buildings: a model of Maiden Newton Signal Box, Great Western Railway, by Rupert Godfrey.

Similarly, there is the equally tedious business of cutting out, without distortion, complicated shapes out of nonferrous metal sheet. Here, the process known as metal etching is now coming to the fore, whereby unwanted metal is eaten away in an acid bath. It is a kind of chemical cutting and filing method, the shape that is wanted is transferred photographically from a drawing to the work piece. People with the right equipment can take a drawing in a special but very simple format and duplicate it in brass. The accuracy depends entirely on the accuracy of the draftsmanship, mitigated by the fact that the drawing can be larger than life size.

The casting processes need both special equipment and special skill, while in the case of the acid-etching process there is some danger involved in do-it-yourself operations. So, does a part produced commercially in this way from a pattern or drawing which one has made oneself count as being built from scratch? If one should want to model competitively the point is important, and is not really resolved at the present time.

One of the most difficult stages in making a model from scratch (or from a kit) is getting a correct finish.

Most British steam express locomotives, from the *North Star* of 1837 to the *Evening Star* of 1961, had colored liveries (whose exact hues are the subject of endless argument), often with complex lining and panelling as well as coats of arms and shaded lettering. Even when the livery was black, it was a special shade called 'Blackberry Black.' Whatever the color, the need to attain perfection is a considerable problem when such complexities are involved.

With a few exceptions, modellers of American steam locomotives have it rather easier when it comes to painting and finish. On the other hand American diesels are notorious for their vivid plumage, while in Britain drab hues and the simplest of plain white insignia are the order of the day. Whatever the style, and whether or not it is wished to portray the model in ex-works or in well-used condition, the difficulties of obtaining a finish which even approximates in appearance to one on an artifact 64 times bigger are considerable. A builder must steel himself to the fact that many failures must precede even moderate success and it is also worth remembering that many paint removers also remove many glues!

In all countries which have model railroading, competitions for scratchbuilt models are held locally and nationally, with the object both of improving standards and of pandering to normal human competitive instincts. In America the location is typically one of the NMRA conventions and in Britain one of the National Model exhibitions.

Little has been said on the other aspects of S gauge and indeed there is little to say. The National Model Railroad Association has track and wheel standards for S gauge and these can be followed with confidence. Light rail for S gauge is the same as heavy rail for HO gauge. For example NMRA Code 80 rail, which means that its height is 0.080 inch, is correct to represent rail 87 times bigger, that is 7 inches in HO scale. This means, in professional terms, that NMRA Code 80 rail is almost equivalent to the 132-pound-per-yard high iron of a trunk route. But if you spike down Code 80 rail on your S-gauge line, the same arithmetic for a $\frac{1}{64}$ scale makes it the near equivalent of the 80 pounds-per-yard rail of some branch lines. Similarly light O-gauge rail can be used for heavy S-gauge iron. This standard coding applies in Britain also, model permanent way specialists Peco of Seaton, Devon, offer Code 100, 80, and 65 rail for building track from scratch, to supplement their famous made-up flexible track, available for other gauges.

Perhaps a tear should be shed that S gauge never made it into the big league, for it is a most attractive size, but at the moment the land of $\frac{3}{16}$-inch scale is like some lovely piece of unspoiled countryside, hard to reach but vastly rewarding to those who get there.

8 O Gauge -- The Great Survivor

Owing to its larger proportions, O gauge has a big following. A model locomotive would weigh eight times as much in O gauge as in HO and all the other items of hardware are proportionately heavy and robust. In the period between the two world wars O gauge was the universal size. Numerous firms and individuals produced vast quantities of locomotives, rolling stock, track, buildings and accessories. Although production of O-gauge material today is relatively small, the immense mass of material created in the 1920s and 1930s has not disappeared. Instead one finds it being passed down to new generations of O-gauge men, who aquire it as secondhand models.

Of course, O gauge is for the perfectionist, the man who really wants to have on his models every visible nut and bolt of the prototype. If that is the aim, then the principles described in the last chapter are the ones that must be applied. Ordinary mortals, however, have to make do with less precise representation, or possibly have other objectives when they re-create the world's railroads in this not quite so miniature size.

As always in the model world, one nominal size hides several separate areas of modelling. It has already been mentioned that one scale ($\frac{1}{4}$ of an inch to 1 foot) is commonly used in America and another (7mm to 1 foot) is normal in the rest of the world. In both sizes

Above and right: On the layout of the Model Railroad Club of Detroit, Michigan: the 'Red Bird' train and its locomotive, based on a Chicago Great Western Railway prototype. It was built by Bill Lenoir.

Left: The demonstration O-scale layout at the Peco Modelrama Southern Railways. In the foreground are narrow-gauge tracks; the use of OO gauge here is exactly correct for the 2-foot 4½-inch gauge Glyn Valley Tramway models on display.

there is a distinction between so-called coarse-scale standards (known in the USA as 'hi-rail') and fine-scale ones. The coarse-scale standards are a legacy from the 'tinplate' standards of pre-World War I days. For many years the wheel standards and track material used for O gauge were to scale not for that size but for 2½-inch gauge. Of course, there are the narrow-gauge sizes too, but these we shall leave until later.

In Britain WS Norris was one of the first O-gauge men to use fine scale. He had to start his own firm – Rocket Precision Ltd – to produce wheels, rail, chairs and many other parts for a magnificent layout. Nowadays the firm of Peco supply ready-to-run fine-scale O-gauge flexible track and points, as well as separate parts. Coarse-scale track parts can still be obtained from the famous old firm of Bonds of Euston Road Ltd, now removed from London's Euston Road to Midhurst,

Sussex, England. In the United States, flexible coarse-scale track is available from Gar-Graves Trackage of New York, while the NMRA has standards for fine and hi-rail wheels and track.

In contrast to HO/OO gauge, O-gauge motive power and rolling stock is not dominated by ready-to-run mass-produced models. Nevertheless they do exist – Lima of Italy have a range which includes a few British models and Rivarossi (also of Italy) are considering entering the O-gauge field. Otherwise, apart from the hand-built or batch-produced brass models built in the Far East for the United States' market, it is a world of small firms offering parts or kits, either white-metal castings or in brass, consisting of shaped pieces of sheet, tube, angle and lost-wax castings. Of course, pieces of sheet, tube, angle and so on, plus machined castings are what real locomotives are built from, so you become a shop foreman before becoming an engine driver.

Advertisements in the specialist O-gauge magazines such as the *O Gauge Gazette*, published by the O Gauge Guild of Britain, or *O Scale Railroading* (published from 6710 Hampton Drive East, Indianapolis, Indiana 46226) tell the tale. Instead of offering a long list of ready-to-run models, they contain things like motors, gears, wheels, small nuts and bolts, metal, plastic and timber. Even fabric for carriage carpeting and upholstery is on the list!

So, in one sense the methods used for O gauge come closer to those used on real railroads than models in the smaller sizes. For example, although the plastic-sleepered track is available, many O-gaugers use rails spiked to actual timber sleepers (with or without chairs, as appropriate) when laying their permanent way. On the other hand, since clockwork was and is a favorite means of propulsion in this size, O-gauge methods of traction are further away from methods used on full-size trains.

In some ways, of course, this use of actual prototype material has its limitations. For example, the London & North Eastern Railway of Britain built its best carriages of teak, finishing them with varnish except for lining and lettering. Long ago it was laid down by a distinguished

Right and far right above: O-gauge fine scale: the layout of WS Norris, the man who pioneered exact-scale permanent way in Britain.

Far right below: The legendary triplex articulated locomotive of the Erie Railroad, the *Matt H Shay* reproduced in O scale.

Next page: A London & North Eastern Railway express hauled by a 4-4-2 awaits the right away in Bromford station on the fabulous O-gauge Bromford & High Peak layout.

LNER O-gauge modeller that 'only one material looks like varnished teak and that is – varnished teak.' A little reflection might cast doubts on this, even leaving aside the fact that superb OO-gauge LNER carriages made of plastic are currently being offered. The reason is a very fundamental one, namely that while a model can be built to scale, nature cannot. In this case the trouble lies in the wide grain of the timber. To make models it is really better to use some close-grained timber such as bass-wood, afterward carefully staining it to give the teak color.

The problem of not being able to scale nature recurs in all sizes of modelling. Its most fundamental manifesta-tion is that the force of gravity remains the same for the model as for the real train. By this is meant that if you dropped an O-gauge LNER Pacific off the actual Forth Bridge at the same time as dropping a real one, they would both reach the water 156 feet below at the same time. Hence, falling a distance of $3\frac{1}{2}$ feet from an O-scale model of the bridge would take an absurdly short time. What we really want for our miniature trains is a minia-ture earth with 'scale' gravity to run them on!

While spectacular disasters of this kind are not a feature of most railroads, real or model, and film makers overcome the difficulty by using slow-motion cameras, the effect also appears in such things as an absurdly

Left: Canadian National Railways 4-8-4: Bernard Gottlieb, who built this model, was the second Honorary Life Member of the National Model Railroad Association.

Right: A superdetail Chicago Great Western 2-10-4 from Michigan.

Below: Two definitive O-gauge models of Great Western rolling stock from the collection of the National Railway Museum. They are an illustration of the sort of detailing both possible and expected in this scale.

Left: The garden-shed layout at the Peco Modelrama. Note the narrow-gauge branch line; the Glyn Valley Tramway stock shown on it is from a line which had a gauge of 2 feet 4½ inches, exactly correct for using OO-gauge track for an O-scale model.

Bottom: Brunel's broad gauge: the Ob7 layout of Bill Stocks' 'Fire Fly' class 2-2-2 running on mixed broad- and standard-gauge cross-sleeper road. Note broad-gauge longitudinal sleeper track in foreground; also fantail caution and disk stop signals on this re-creation of the Great Western in Queen Victoria's time.

Below: Simple but effective – the Pacific Eastern Lines of the late Butler Jack of Sacramento.

quick drop of a model signal arm or the acceleration of a train in a few revolutions of the wheels. The apparently stronger force of gravity in a model world is also the reason for relatively higher speeds being possible on curves, or the possibility of running a reciprocating steam freight locomotive at a scale 250mph, say, without stripping the rods. In the model, only restraining hands on the controls, rather than the implacable forces of nature, prevent such unrealistic occurrences.

The fact that nature cannot be scaled is also a handicap for live-steam model locomotives in a size as small as O gauge. It is certainly possible – spirit or gas-fired steam locomotives were available on a ready-to-run basis in the recent past and may well be so again – but the size of grit in model coal-ash is the same size as it is in full size. Moreover, halving the size of a model boiler means reducing the surface area four times, but reducing the volume eight times. Therefore, in proportion to the heat stored, the heat lost increases with very noticeable effects. Live steam is better done in still bigger sizes.

On the other hand, O gauge is a size which suits the reproduction of one very enchanting facet of railroad operation very well. Traditional mechanical signalling is now vanishing from the world's big railroads, but that is no reason why it should vanish from ours. Whereas modern electrical signalling is actually easier to install in small sizes such as HO and N than in O gauge because of availability of equipment, proper mechanical signalling is not. Rods and wires to work points and

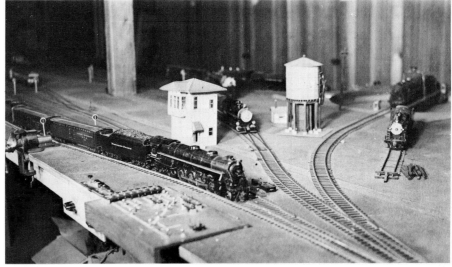

signals are far too fragile in smaller sizes, but in this scale the mechanical delights of old-fashioned signalling are easily possible.

In America most smaller stations did not have interlocking signals, whereas in Britain and in most countries where British influence predominated, fully interlocked signalling was mandatory at even the least important places. So, taking the British principles of mechanical signalling as our model, we begin working out how they should be applied. The result, it has been said, is more like poetry than engineering. The rods and wires bring the control of all points and signals to a common set of levers grouped together in a frame. A system of transverse bars interlock the levers so that conflicting lever movements cannot be made. In detail, the objects of interlocking are as follows:

1. To ensure that a signalman shall be unable to pull off, that is clear, a signal until any points concerned are correctly set.
2. To make it impossible to clear at the same time two signals which may lead to a collision between trains.
3. To make it impossible to move any points connected with, or leading to, the line over which a train is moving until the signal governing that train is set at danger.

Semaphore signal arms are normally horizontal in the stop or caution position – a symbolic barring of the way – and either go up or down to an oblique angle for all clear. The siting of home, distant, starting, junction, backing, calling-on and shunting signals has much akin to composing some great musical symphony.

Literally musical and intimately linked with all this is the famous block system with its single-beat bell codes connecting adjacent signal boxes. On any layout depicting the steam-age scene which is worth its salt should be heard that always thrilling signal of four beats, meaning 'is line clear for express passenger train or breakdown crane going to clear the line?'; or, the even more exciting signal of 12 beats, given as two, pause, five, pause, five, meaning 'train running away on wrong line!' Miniature block instruments and block bells were, until a few years ago, available from Hornby of England, but the construction of replicas would not be beyond anyone possessing a little electrical ingenuity. Perhaps the only feature of steam-age signalling that is difficult to arrange in O gauge is the oil lighting of signal lights – but electric lighting using either fiber-optics or 'grain of wheat' bulbs is a reasonable substitute. A very good starting point for apprentice signalling enthusiasts would be the handbook *Railway Signalling and Communications*, published by the Railway Gazette of London – but it would have to be a secondhand copy.

One very basic structure which is almost totally neglected by modellers is real superdetail miniature permanent way. This again could be exactly duplicated in O gauge. Even a simple turnout (often called a 'single lead' or 'half-shunt' in full size) should have the two switches and the crossing as separate units, connected by so-called closure rails. One almost never sees the rail joints in the right places. Furthermore, if the radius is less (in O-gauge equivalent terms) than 15 feet, in Britain it is a Ministry of Transport regulation that a check rail should be provided on the inside of the curve. This also applies to plain line. Also rarely seen in model form are what are called switch diamonds, that

Above: David Jenkinson's model of the Settle & Carlisle line shown under construction; the picture, besides showing what can be expected when this layout is completed, illustrates very well the principles of baseboard construction.

Right: The Midland Railway exhibit in the Derby Municipal Museum takes the form of this superb fine-scale model railroad of definitive quality. The view shows Kirtley station at a busy period.

Next page: The erstwhile O-gauge display layout at Modelland, New Romney, set up by Captain Howey of the Romney, Hythe & Dymchurch Railway.

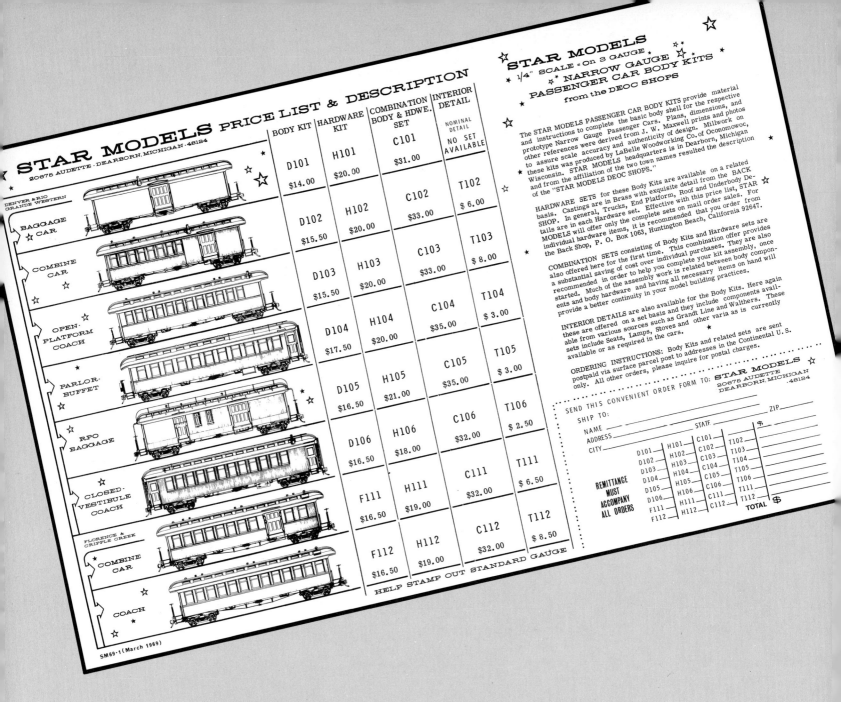

is, diamond crossings where the obtuse crossings in the center have to be worked like two pairs of switches, according to which line is in use – although these are mandatory in full size for the circumstances which often apply on model layouts. It is a shame to see fabulous superdetail locomotives from an otherwise perfect layout running on permanent way that is just packed with mistakes. The professional handbook *British Railway Track*, covering both bullhead and flat-bottom rail practice, is both very readable and an excellent starting point. It is published by the Permanent Way Institution at 27 Leawood Road, Fleet, Hants, GU1 38AN, England.

As for HO gauge, narrow-gauge offshoots and derivitives abound. Indeed, the scale known as On3, for models of 3-foot gauge prototypes, is better provided for in America than is O-gauge proper. Kits for almost every vehicle ever possessed by that legendary Denver and Rio Grande Empire in Colorado, as well as numerous other lines, are on the market. The exact scale gauge of ¾ of an inch is used and in many other ways the material offered, mostly in kit form, is consistently of top quality. Apart from brass models which are occasionally available (at rather high cost), ready-to-run does not exist, but aids such as lost-wax castings take much of the pain out of the process of building from scratch.

In Britain, O-gauge models to run on OO-gauge track have a considerable following. Although in precise terms the equivalent scale gauge of this combination represents 28½ inches, a rare but not entirely unknown figure in the world's railroads, it is in fact used for models of narrow-gauge lines of gauges from 23½–30 inches. Peco of England not only do correct large-sleepered track and points for this size but also, and unusually for them, several locomotives in kit form. George Mellor of Rhos-on-Sea, North Wales, also caters for this market.

There is a reason for the popularity of both of these sizes. A full-size O-gauge layout needs a really large room – for instance an express train should be some 16–20 feet long in this size. Narrow-gauge trains have not only in general fewer coaches, but each coach is a good deal shorter; accordingly, 5 feet is a generous amount to allow. This makes all the difference and to some extent allows the modeller to make the best of both worlds – the satisfying size of O scale coupled to the space-saving properties of smaller gauges.

Enough has been said to show that O gauge is really the size for the specialist, the man to whom correct detail is as important as overall appearance. Moreover this detail should and usually does follow full-size practice, not only in outward form but in method of construction and use, more closely than in the smaller sizes.

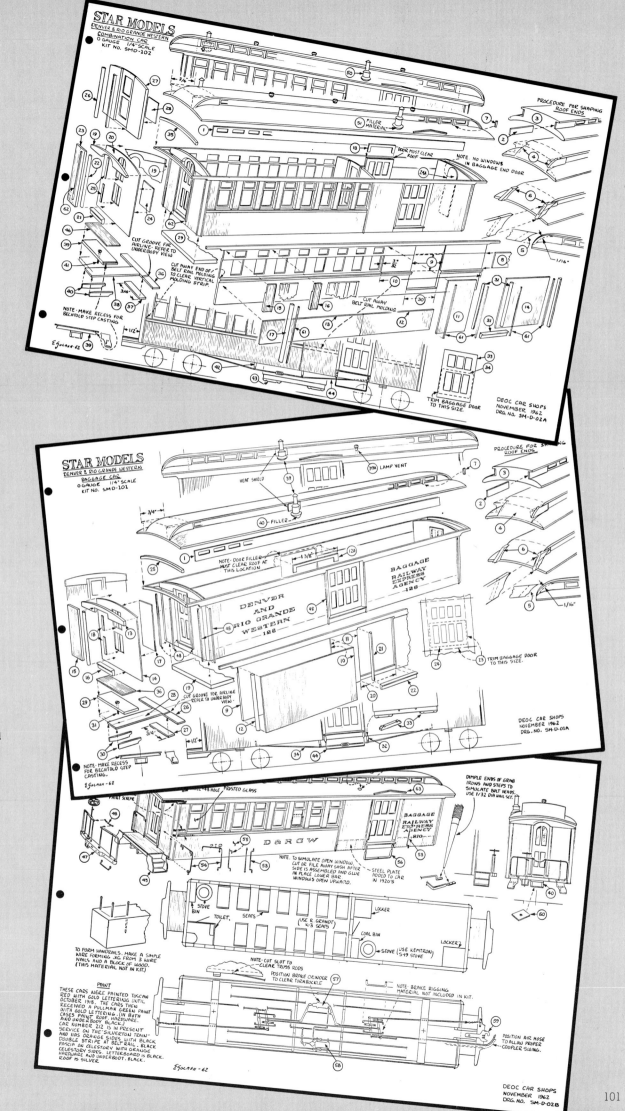

Star Models of Dearborn, Michigan, USA, produced this leaflet describing typical components for making up a superb range of narrow-gauge passenger-car kits. The prices are those of several years ago.

Left: Nigel MacMillan of Glasgow runs this delightful 4-6-2T decked out in the royal blue of the Caledonian Railway. The track is the old coarse scale material.

Top: The late Dennis Allenden of West Virginia brought to life on his side of the Atlantic some of the quaint delights of vintage French railroading such as this 2-4-2 'long-boiler'-type express locomotive.

Above: Denver & Rio Grande Western narrow-gauge parlor-buffet-observation car; the part completed kit is by Star Models.

9 Outdoor Scenic Railroads

In this business of reproducing railroads in miniature, a frontier is crossed when, instead of making a model railroad on a baseboard one goes out-of-doors into the garden, and builds a railroad on a grade cut out of or built up on the ground. In fact, this has been done even in N gauge, but the problems begin to multiply in a size where, for example, the tiniest of fallen leaves will derail a train. Ground-level layouts involve their owners in a continuous and fairly titanic struggle against the disruptive forces of nature but in sizes below 1 gauge (1¾ inches) the contest is a little too unequal for most people. Of course many excellent 1-gauge layouts have been laid on baseboards either indoors or outdoors, but one could reasonably regard 1 gauge in this context as a stretched version of O gauge. Alternatively an indoor-type layout on a raised baseboard can be built outdoors, to take advantage of the extra space available. This is an excellent ploy which has been used by such famous enthusiasts as Cecil J Allen (who did it in O gauge) and Victor B Harrison. Harrison planted privet hedges to disguise the stilts which supported his quite superb 1-gauge line.

It is sad to relate that outdoor ground-level scenic model railroads are one of the most neglected areas of model railroads, yet, at the same time, one with great possibilities. Steam and even diesel traction are definitely practicable to supplement electric and clock-work propulsion, while outdoor operation is the rule rather than the exception. Live steam outdoors is certainly the ultimate in scenic model railroads.

Although steam has now vanished (except as a tourist attraction) from most advanced countries, it still has an unbelievable hold on the imagination of men. This is illustrated by a count on the shelves of most model shops where it will be found that steam power will far outnumber any other. Of course, the model steam power shown will mostly be pseudo to the extent that it will in reality be electrically driven. However real model live steam, which we have noted as a great rarity in the HO/OO world and which is occasionally found in O gauge, really comes into its own with 1 gauge and upward.

Below: The late Cecil J Allen, the distinguished railroad author, observes operations on his famous garden railway at Hatch End, Hertfordshire, now long dismantled.

These large-gauge sizes of model railroads are of course those with which the movement began, as described in Chapter 2. Before 1914 they were the most popular sizes, but for a long period since then big model trains have been in a decline. For this reason, and contrary to the situation in O gauge, only a modest amount of material, and at rarity prices, comes up on the secondhand market. A faithful few, by dint of do-it-yourself methods, have kept these scales alive and their reward has been that during the last decade there has been something of a revival commercially – which, as in the early days, is centered in the German town of Nuremberg.

A few years ago Maerklin put on the market a small 1-gauge range, which now includes a very nice German class '38' ex-Prussian 4-6-0. Unfortunately the small scale of production results in higher prices than are usual for commercial model trains. Supplementing these is a series of 1-gauge, live-steam, gas-fired, model locomotives currently made by a firm called Aster. A few years ago Fulgureaux of Lausanne marketed a series of German ex-Bavarian Railways 4-6-2s and other types which (at a fairly high price) were not only steam propelled but electrically controlled. A magnificent collection of these fabulous creations operates on the 1-gauge layout of the Model Railway Club of Basle, Switzerland, situated in a large building in the center of the city's main railroad marshalling yards.

Top: The long-existing and pioneer outdoor gauge-1 layout of Victor B Harrison at Bishops Stortford. A live-steam model of record-breaking Great Western Railway 4-4-0 *City of Truro* is taking the through road at Lone Pine station. Note signal box of aluminum simulating timber construction.

Left: Another view of CJ Allen's railroad, this time a previous layout at Barnet, showing the main terminus. The young Geoffrey Freeman Allen (himself now a well-known writer on railroads) looks on. Note the line on the right running into the storage shed and workshop.

Controlled live steam is surprisingly easy to arrange. As long as 15 years ago a team – Messrs Getgood, Mills and Thompson – demonstrated in public at the Manchester (England) Model Railway Exhibition a layout on which electrically fired and electrically controlled steam locomotives ran and shunted impeccably while being driven from the line-side. The system was of elemental simplicity, but functioned extremely well.

Recently a number of pioneers have managed to widen the concept by making the locomotives independent of contact wire or rail. Their ideas cover the *radio* control of *gas*-fired live steam. Just around the corner for them is a two-way radio link by means of which information concerning the water level, steam pressure and other essential data is fed back to the driver. Even without remote control gear a ready-to-run gauge-1 steam locomotive costs the same as perhaps 20 HO-gauge electric ones.

Electric traction is equally possible, but the oxidation of rails which occurs outdoors can lead to contact difficulties. Battery-powered electric locomotives were used 40 years ago by that master of gauge-1 railroads, the late VB Harrison. With better batteries and radio control available now, the method should be a winner.

VB Harrison was a pioneer of control systems intended for his fleet of steam locomotives. A control wagon was attached to the locomotive, as it gathered speed air pressure was generated by a pump. If speed rose too

Left: A corner of Bill Stocks' enchanting Heatherfield Light Railway. Note the 'Crampton'-type locomotive in the center.

Right: Electrically controlled live-steam Royal Bavarian State Railway 4-6-2 in gauge 1 by Wilag of Germany.

Below: Note how a delightful garden rockery is improved by the presence of an 'Emett'-style railroad – in this case the Heatherfield Light Railway.

Left: The train shed/ terminus: Marylebone Station (having, quite unusually for the model world, *more* platforms than the prototype) in the early and railroad-conscious days of the Bekonscot Model Village at Beaconsfield, Buckinghamshire, England.

Below left: Locomotive No 9 *Lucy* arrives at King's Gap station on the Heatherfield line; note the attention to detail including the pedestal-mounted historical relic.

Below: The entrance to the train shed/terminus on Donald Neale's gauge-O outdoor Kirtley layout.

high, pressure also rose and a little control cylinder on the locomotive shut the regulator; as speed fell, the regulator opened again. Over the undulating grades of the designer's system, this gave fairly realistic operation.

Clockwork flourished for many years in these big sizes and such details as sophisticated two-speed mechanisms 'braked and reversed from the track side' were available. Alas, such delights are no longer made, but a few devotees still keep and run working examples of this elegant type of motive power in its largest size.

Diesel-electric traction really is fairly difficult. Only one genuine diesel-electric model locomotive is known to exist – made in gauge 1 by the television producer Robin Symes-Schutzmann of London.

The next scale above that associated with gauge 1 is gauge 2, that is, $2\frac{1}{2}$-inch gauge, scale $\frac{1}{2}$ an inch or $\frac{17}{32}$ of an inch to one foot and this still remains in decline, but narrow-gauge models to this scale are prospering. For do-it-yourself people, a scale of 16mm (approximately $\frac{5}{8}$ of an inch) to 1 foot on O-gauge track is popular when used for satisfyingly large 2-foot gauge models. The so-called coarse-scale wheel and track material, which was for so long all that was available for O gauge, suits narrow-gauge modelling much better than standard gauge.

That something like this should be attempted is no surprise because of course anyone who is prepared to undertake the task of making a model railroad from scratch is not bound by what commercial manufacturers might happen to offer. However the enterprising German firm of Lehmann has developed Lehmann Gross Bahn (Lehmann Big Railway), which consists of really huge plastic narrow-gauge trains running on

immensely solid and corrosion-resistant 1-gauge track.

All the models in the LGB range are excellent, the bigger ones are accurate and superbly detailed scale electrically-driven models of Austrian, German and Swiss narrow-gauge locomotives (steam, diesel and electric) plus other equipment. The flagship of the range is a miniature edition of one of the delightful and complex 'baby crocodile' articulated outside-frame rod-drive electric locomotives of the Swiss Rhaetian Railway, familiar to those who visit such places as Davos and St Moritz.

The raison d'être of full-size narrow-gauge trains is an ability to go round very sharp curves. This characteristic has been passed on by Lehmann to these models so that these big trains can run on layouts in quite ordinary-sized rooms using curves as sharp as 25 inches in radius. The trains are also suitable for temporary layouts laid on the floor; Lehmann publicity shows an elephant standing rather gingerly on a length of their track, so demonstrating that the normal bugbear of track laid on the floor – damage by being walked on – need not be feared. Of course, LGB railroad material is specially suitable for use outdoors.

To an even larger scale, but by no means resulting in any larger hardware, has come a live-steam model of Stephenson's Rocket. Recently, the English firm of Hornby has placed on the market, complete with plastic track, a $3\frac{1}{2}$-inch gauge version of this most famous of all locomotives which 150 years ago introduced intercity rail travel to the inhabitants of Liverpool and Manchester.

Alas, workers in $3\frac{1}{2}$-inch gauge are seduced by a totally different concept of the hobby which is described in the next chapter; this seems rather a pity, as a $3\frac{1}{2}$-inch

Right: Lehmann Gross Bahn – the fantastic range of large-scale narrow-gauge LGB equipment.

Below: A typical LGB train set laid outdoors.

(or 2½-inch gauge) main-line train would be extremely attractive running in a nicely laid-out garden. Perhaps the success of LGB's narrow-gauge trains might one day tempt them, or a rival, to offer main-line ones of similar size. In fact, to the scale of LGB trains the standard-gauge equivalent is almost exactly 2½ inches. For the scratchbuilder castings, aluminum flat-bottom rail and other parts are already available. Scale 2½-inch gauge bullhead rail and chairs were used for many years in Britain to make what was euphemistically called 'standard' O-gauge track and are actually still on sale new, although of the vast quantities made much will still exist and can be acquired secondhand.

Having reviewed what is available and what are the possibilities in the way of railroad hardware for the big train size, we come to the building of the line. It should be noted that cutting and embankment slopes in normal ground should be no steeper than 1½ feet horizontally to 1 foot vertically, and they should be

carefully turfed or sown to keep the soil from being washed on to the line. Embankments need compacting either artificially with a roller, or naturally by being left to settle for a season. So much full-size permanent way work is a kind of overscale gardening that it should be no surprise that model railroads at ground level outdoors have all the penalties and rewards of garden ownership. With an extraordinary perception of outdoor model railroaders' future needs, the Japanese have, over the last few centuries, developed the ancient art of Bonsai that is, the growing of miniature trees. This craft, together with certain miniature species of trees and other rockery plants, can make a special delight of the environs of an outdoor railroad.

Generally speaking the construction of the roadbed should follow garden path techniques, with the alternatives of hardcore or concrete to be considered. With the former, although naturally the topsoil would be dug out, weeds still have to be eliminated. Difficulties

Left: Denver & Rio Grande Western 'reefer' by LGB.

Below: Adapted from LGB parts by Charles Snell of Cos Cob, Connecticut, is this enchanting 2-6-2 + 0-4-0 Yankee-style powered-tender steam locomotive.

with the latter are associated with the need to take
account of expansion and contraction.

As most people know, real railroad track is not
normally fixed down in any way, it just sits down on and
is held in place by the ballast. Exceptions occur across
some bridges and in a few places where conventional
permanent way has been replaced by concrete slab
track. With model track, the difference is that the rails
are relatively much less flexible, even in these large
scales. If one takes, for example, a 2-foot length of
gauge-1 track and lifts it at one end it will remain almost
flat. On the other hand if you take a 60-foot length of
full-size track and similarly lift it at one end, the far end
will remain flat on the ground. The result is that a level
model track is not achieved by packing up the ballast
but instead by making sure the rails receive no permanent kinks or bends. The best way of doing this is to
lay what is a comparatively rigid track on a rigid
foundation, with ballast laid for purely cosmetic reasons.

A major problem with outdoor railroads is the buildings. If timber is used for the many structures which are
made of timber in full size, then they are usually not
robust enough to stand up to the weather. In fact, the
life of a scale timber building is typically reduced in
proportion to the scale to which it is built. Suitable
plastic materials can be substituted with some fairly
indefinable loss of realism, but if real timber is used the
buildings in question must be brought indoors when not
in use.

Metal structures can reasonably be made using nonferrous metals as a substitute for iron and steel. The

problem is that on ground-level structures like signal
posts, catenary supports and even the more fragile sort
of station verandas and footbridges are very vulnerable
to damage by marauders of both the two- and four-
legged kind. Building an outdoor model railroad
means finding out the hard way about the surprisingly
prolific and destructive wildlife of one's particular
locality!

Scale buildings made from conventional permanent
building materials can be very nice, although successful
scale brickwork and unrendered stonework is very
difficult to achieve. One must also say that if they are not
made with care they can be quite ghastly, but since
construction is cheap and the broken bits that should
follow dissatisfaction are useful for extending the
roadbed, this should not cause too many problems.

One most important feature of an outdoor model railroad is the indoor part because, whatever may be the
case as regards the buildings, there is no doubt at all
that the locomotives and cars must be brought indoors
for storage. Of course this rolling stock can be carried
in and out, the best solution is to have a line into a railroad shed or room, in which there can be a terminal
station, or possibly just sidings.

Outdoor large-scale model railroads (except for the
LGB range) are not for the beginner. The number of
man-hours needed to build an acceptable layout is
several times greater than is needed to build one in
HO/OO gauge. However the faithful few who practice
this facet of model railroading are invariably well
satisfied that all the trouble is worthwhile.

10 Live-Steam Locomotives

In the last chapter we crossed a barrier into building real ground-level railroads – in this chapter we cross another. This time it is into driving real locomotives, and from a world where electricity is the norm and steam rare to one where steam is the norm and electricity (and internal combustion) rare.

It is also the story of 'Curly' Lawrence, the founder of the live-steam movement, who wrote some 3000 articles on building what he called 'little locomotives,' between 1922 and his death in 1967. An unbroken weekly series written under the pseudonym 'LBSC' appeared in the magazine *Model Engineer* from 1923–1959. 'LBSC' wrote mainly for the beginner, who had the ambition to build himself a real steam locomotive fired by coal. He covered the subject from equipping the workshop to laying the track, not forgetting driving, firing and even buying and selling. The articles were to the point, crystal clear, wise, intimate, gritty and often very funny. He provided instruction for building 85 steam locomotive designs; castings and parts for many of them are still available.

His successors, such as Don Young (of *Live Steam* and *Locomotives Large and Small*), Martin Evans, Keith Wilson and Ted Martin (of the *Model Engineer*) have built on the sound foundations laid down by Lawrence's work. The fruit of all these labors has been thousands of steam locomotives built by the members of hundreds of

Left: The size of this 5-inch gauge 0-6-0T, which is modelled on a Great Western locomotive, illustrates how the choice of a narrow-gauge prototype produces a very large model. The original ran on the 2-foot 6-inch gauge Welshpool & Llanfair Light Railway in Wales, while the model is seen here on the track of the Rugby Model Engineering Club.

Below left: *Tugboat Annie*, designed and built for the 2½-inch gauge by LBSC. It was his answer to the fleet of full-size Pacifics designed for the Southern Railway by Oliver Bulleid. *Tugboat Annie* has four cylinders, the inside pair set at 45 degrees to the outside ones, but with their valves worked by an ingenious 4-to-2 system of rocking levers visible in the photograph.

Right: Five-inch gauge railroads can be laid on the ground, but the knees-in-mouth contortions involved do not suit everybody. Sir Berkeley Sheffield, Bart, runs his stretched Great Northern style Atlantic-turned-Pacific on his own line of this size at Normanby Park, Lincolnshire.

Next page: A 40-year-old 4-4-2, built by Jack Woods, on the track of the British Columbia Society of Model Engineers.

Inset next page: The live-steam scene: the driver of a 3½-inch gauge LNER 4-6-0 class B1 express locomotive pulls away from a signal stop under the control of a cautionary yellow light. The scene is the Kinver track of the West Midlands Model Engineering Society of England.

live-steam clubs to the gauges of 3½, 4¾ and 5 inches and to scales of ¾, 1 and 1¹⁄₁₆ inches to the foot. The 4¾ inches to 1 inch scale combination is normal in the United States and Canada, 5 inches to 1¹⁄₁₆ inches scale elsewhere – again a reflection of uncertainty as to whether to choose a simple scale or a simple gauge. Of course, in sizes where so much is do-it-yourself, the problems which arise over variations in scale and gauge are not serious ones.

In order to become the owner of a live-steam locomotive, the first step might reasonably be to subscribe to one of the periodicals mentioned, while the second might be to join a club. A worldwide list of live-steam clubs is given in the author's recent book, *How to Drive a Steam Locomotive* (Architectural Press, London). Most clubs welcome new members and offer them excellent help and advice.

With the aid of constructional articles from the magazines plus a little advice from fellow club members, many people without previous experience have built satisfactory live-steam locomotives. While every facility in the way of castings parts and tools are available, it must be said that even the simplest type of passenger-hauling steam locomotive would take at least two years of spare time to construct. Furthermore, the minimum equipment needed would be a robust metal-turning lathe, power drill, plus the usual hand tools, sets of taps and dies, work-bench, welding and brazing equipment.

Recently, kits of finished parts have come onto the market for the first time. It is noted that a kit to build a 2-6-0 American type in 3½-inch gauge is being offered at $3000 (£1500) by a Japanese firm of model airplane-engine builders.

Next page: *Oliver Bulleid:* a 5-inch gauge live-steam model of one of the Southern Railway 4-6-2s so disapproved of by LBSC. It was built by the late Mr Cushing of Rainham, Kent, and is an incredible *tour-de-force* of model engineering in reproducing the complex mechanism of the prototype.

Above: *Stormy Petrel:* a 3½-inch gauge Great Western 4-6-0 built to LBSC's 'County' class design, displayed on a length of scale track. This would be quite incapable of supporting the kind of loads she is able to haul.

Below: The smallest size of locomotive that will reasonably haul a live adult driver is represented by this 'Green Arrow' class London & North Eastern Railway 2-6-2, running on the 2½-inch gauge. It is another of LBSC's designs.

Of course it is possible to commission a locomotive to be built from scratch from a reputable builder, but the snag is that some 1000 man-hours of skilled work have to be paid for and one does not need to be an economist to realize what that means. Buying a second-hand locomotive tends to be as tricky as horse dealing. LBSC laid down the rule that one should not part with money until one had tried one's purchase in steam. However one acquires a model there is an incredible fascination in watching these real steam puffers burning real coal on tiny grates. Control is no problem because in these sizes you drive yourself, generally sitting astride on a flat car with footrests. The track would be raised, multigauge, and usually arranged in an oval to give runs of any length for which the locomotive has the power. The building and operation of these loco-motives is not restricted to the rich and therefore, because the tracks are costly both in space and material, the clubs perform this task. Some clubs have bought or leased land and built a track, clubroom and workshop, others operate in public parks, giving rides to children in return for their accommodation. Live-steam clubs with tracks number some 60 in the United States, 12 in Canada, 120 in Britain, 18 in Australasia and 10 in southern Africa. The movement is just beginning to take shape in other industrial countries such as Japan, France, Germany, and The Netherlands.

Curiously enough, the steady development of the hobby has been completely unaffected by the end of steam on the world's railroads. The only detectable effect seems to be just that those who preferred new product as a prototype have either to settle for models with historic significance or to design and build a model of a locomotive that might have been developed in full size, had steam continued.

Returning to the tracks themselves, there are two main schools of thought in respect of construction. The first advocates the more expensive method of spiking or screwing nonferrous near-scale flat-bottom rail to cross sleepers supported 30 inches above ground level by timber, steel or concrete longitudinals resting on concrete pillars. In essence, this type of track follows the design of the legendary Polar route, the line which belonged to Curly Lawrence. He described all its stages from survey to operation in his usual charming style in the *Model Engineer* in 1934–36. His track is still visible alongside the London–Brighton main line on the up side just south of Purley Oaks station.

The second school follows an equally hallowed example, that of the track belonging to the Society of Model and Experimental Engineers of London which, in portable form, has been the principal feature of many British model-engineering exhibitions since before World War I. Here, steel flats are set on edge and spaced with tie bolts and spacing pieces; cross sleepers are dispensed with. In some cases the track formed in this way is strong enough to be self-supporting between uprights, in others independent longitudinals are used. The advantage is either that of cheapness or the ability to easily provide gauges additional to the normal 2½, 3½ and 5 inches. The disadvantage of steel-strip tracks is that the hard sharp-edged flats are unkind to cast-iron locomotive wheels. Steel tires, as used in full size, are unusual in small practice.

As with most types of monorail, points are a problem and usually some form of turntable or traverser is used. Running connections would just be feasible but no one in Britain seems to have achieved them. Neither, apparently, have any appeared in recent years in the United States, although the New England Live Steamers' Club at Danvers, Massachusetts, USA, had them at one time. A few clubs, notably Derby and Ickenham, have ground-level tracks, but this involves certain problems both with stability because of the narrowness of the gauge and also with comfort because of the inevitable lowness of the seats. Yoga training is an essential for riding ground-level passenger tracks in this size, but of course points and crossings, even though mixed gauge, can reasonably easily be provided.

As points are so difficult on raised tracks, the typical layout is of elemental simplicity, oval or hourglass in shape. Double ovals with an overpass are a possibility, exciting because the vertical clearance at the bridge must be sufficient for footboards below rail level to clear heads well above. Other railroad features can be more easily provided; signalling is important when several locomotives may be out on the track at once and here we run the gamut of full-size practice from 'permissive block' (a euphemism for being without signalling) to automatic four-aspect color-light signal-ling with track circuits. A station complete with plat-forms, footbridge and, hopefully, the usual conveni-

Right: LBSC's fame as a designer spread far and away beyond the places where he lived, that is, in Surrey, England and, for a time, Greenwich, Connecticut. This 5-inch gauge 4-4-0 to his 'Maid of Kent' drawings was built in Holland by Mr A Schoenmakers.

Below: An LBSC *Pamela* 4-6-2 in Western Australia.

ences, is important since if conditions are right and safety is adequately covered, club funds can be augmented by offering rides to the public. In fact, many sites have been made available by local authorities on condition that this amenity is provided.

One club, the North London, whose track is at Colney Heath, has gone so far as to fit water troughs and in spite of very different hydrodynamics in the smaller scale, they function satisfactorily. Elsewhere, when a long nonstop run is operated, cans of water are exchanged on the fly like mailbags or single-line tokens in full size. On English tracks, rolling stock is almost invariably confined to the flat trucks with footboards which carry the passengers. In America this is not so; many live-steam buffs hang some scale box-cars and a caboose or perhaps some varnish, that is passenger cars, on to the couplers of their driving car, making up a caboose hop, limited, drag or hotshot as appropriate. So, unless he lives in the very wild and remote parts of the Anglo-Saxon world, anyone having a steam locomotive is within reach of a type of model railroading which is very different. It is more realistic in some ways because you have real steam and coal and drive your own train, less in others because the track layout is usually of elemental simplicity as described.

What is it like to have a day out on one of these lines? First, the locomotive has either to be taken down from its pedestal or else extracted from its hiding place, cleaned and carried out to the car. A 3½-inch gauge 4-6-0, weighing without tender say 70 pounds, can easily be lifted by one person; 5-inch gauge locomotives, unless very small, need more than one person. Next, all the paraphernalia of a miniature running shed has to be collected, fire irons, coal, kindling, two kinds of oil, tool box, steam-raising blower, a few spare parts; then away to the track.

Most live-steam clubs provide steam-raising sidings connected to the main line by a traverser or turntable

Right: Bill Fenton's 3½-inch gauge 'Hudson' rides a magnificent trestle bridge on the track of the British Columbia Society of Model Engineers.

Below: A Southern Pacific 'Pacific' does the rounds of the Golden Gate Line Steamers' track in Oakland, California.

Above: A 4¾-inch gauge logging locomotive built by Ken Roeh of Yakima, Washington, USA.

Right: A green-painted 3½-inch gauge 4-6-4 Hudson locomotive teeters across a high and somewhat fragile-looking trestle on the track of the Golden Gate Live Steamers.

and it is on one of these that operations begin. Perhaps the most amazing thing about these little locomotives is the way coal will burn on a tiny grate which may be as small as $1\frac{1}{2}$ by $2\frac{1}{2}$ inches and produce sufficient energy to drive them along hauling loads several times greater than scale. However, one effect that cannot be reproduced is the natural draft upon which full-size locomotives depend for raising steam. Forced draft has to be provided, either by an electrically-driven blower adapted to suck from the chimney or by compressed air applied to a nozzle in an extension chimney. After a check to see if there is water in the boiler, the blower is set up, switched on, the system is ignited with a scrap of paraffin-soaked rag and the first wood or charcoal is fed in, then coal, to build up a fire. The fuel must be broken up into pieces which will enter a scale fire-hole door.

Raising steam in these sizes is a fairly rapid operation. Boilers are almost invariably 100 percent copper with excellent conductivity and the volume of water is several thousand times less than full size. Where in full-size steam raising one allows hours, in miniature one allows the same number of minutes, perhaps seven or eight, in fact barely time to get around the bearings with an oil can and fill the cylinder lubricator with that strange treacly substance known as superheated steam oil. Now comes perhaps the best moment when the needle of the pressure gauge lifts off the zero stop pin, the artificial draft can be dispensed with and the engine's own blower turned on. Then and there she comes alive with a strong personality all her own.

A word with the track steward to check that all is clear and a short warming-up run in the sidings to clear condensed steam out of the cylinders completes the preparations. The locomotive is then moved on to the main line and coupled up to the flat cars which form the train. The driver and passengers can now clamber on and then, in the words of the originator of the movement:

'You see the water is near the top of the gauge and the fire has just burnt through. She is just under working pressure, 80 pounds and the blower is on a little. Sit straight on the flat car and don't fidget about and you'll ride quite safely; a cyclist rides on a narrower gauge; I bet you never thought of that. Don't forget that the handles on her footplate work the same as those on big sister, but that handle sticking through, like a damper, works the by-pass cock as the little engine feeds her boiler with a pump.

Open the regulator very steady until you feel her pull, then give her just a little more, but don't let her slip. Bad enginemanship causes more slipping than big cylinders. Now you have to do the fireman's job as well. Don't notch up yet but shut the blower-valve and pop a bit on the fire whilst she is puffing hard, a shovelful each side and one at the back. Open the regulator a little more and she will gather speed; now you can notch up as the blast has pulled the fire through. The water is dropping in the glass and she is just going to blow off, so shut the by-pass and let the lot go into the boiler. This will hold the steam pressure down for a minute or so, but as the water gets up near the top nut, open the by-pass a little and endeavour to keep the water at that level. The fire will now be fully incandescent so she will blow off again as the feed is reduced; so open the door and pop on some more coal same as before. Now you are all set for a record run if you like. The mechanical lubricator will take care of the oiling and all you have to do is to judge how often to fire her and keep her to a safe speed.'

Concentration: a 5-inch gauge Midland Railway 'Crimson Rambler' type compound 4-4-0 at speed.

Left: *Mount Kilimanjaro* on loan to the Hilton Valley Railway.

Below left: Porters Hill Railway: a Hunslet 0-4-0 enters the station.

Below: The running number of this Atlantic represents its date of construction. It is now owned by Ernie Allen of New Westminster, British Columbia.

Bottom: Own your own 'Streak'; a 5-inch gauge model of a London & North Eastern A4 class streamline 4-6-2 on passenger duty.

As you will realize, driving and firing these little machines is no sinecure. First, you are doing tasks which in full size are allotted to two men. Second, with such a relatively minute volume of fire and water present the steam-production cycle can deteriorate very quickly. George Barlow, Operating Manager of the Romney, Hythe & Dymchurch Railway, whose locomotives ⅓ full size come half way between the little ones we have been discussing and full size, finds that handling them comes easier to drivers with miniature experience than to those with full size. Every pleasure has its price and after the run there are the chores to carry out; drop the fire, clear the smokebox, sweep the tubes and clean up. There are other locomotives and their running to observe, endless discussions to be engaged in on the relative merits of Churchward and Gresley, Walschaerts and Stephenson, compounds and simples, Welsh steam coal and Yorkshire hards, and numerous other aspects of railroading.

A milestone in the progress of the live-steam cause was reached with the publication for the first time of a magazine which deals exclusively with the construction and operation of little steam locomotives. Previously, such publications as the *Model Engineer* (in Britain) and *Live Steam* (in the United States) have given good coverage to their locomotive side but, of course, many other things mechanical had to have coverage also. The first issue of the new magazine contains the start of serial instructions to build a narrow-gauge 0-4-0T quarry locomotive in 5-inch gauge (and 7¼-inch gauge) size, as well as an archetypal British 4-4-0, the 'Glen' class from the old North British Railway in Scotland. This latter is also for 5-inch gauge, but will be very different in design and concept. It is understood that future projects will cover locomotive practice on both sides of the Atlantic. *Locomotives Large and Small* appears quarterly and is published by Don Young Designs, of Bardonela, Adgestone, Sandown, Isle of Wight, England. The magazine is available worldwide only by postal subscription.

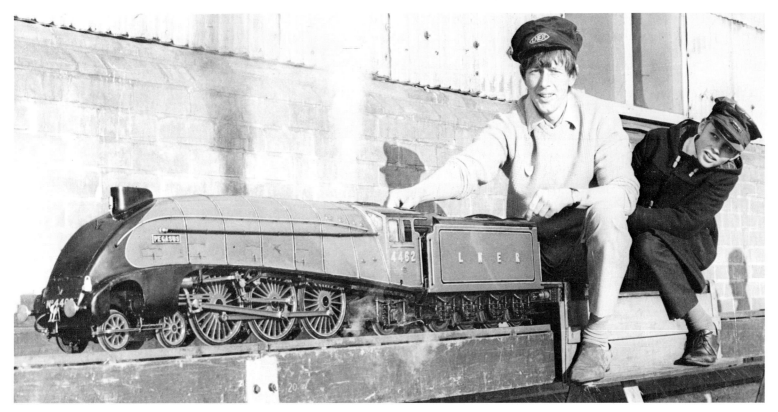

11 Miniature Railroads

In the last chapter we saw how in the smallest size of coal-fired steam-powered passenger hauling railroads, it is normal to sacrifice realism, in everything except the locomotives, by putting the track on stilts and using totally unrailroadlike rolling stock. We also saw how the total realism of the locomotive made this sacrifice worthwhile. A more balanced spread of realism of the railroad can be achieved by going bigger still, to sizes where one rides on the locomotive, which in turn rides on real permanent way laid on proper stone ballast. The term 'miniature' rather than 'model' is the accustomed usage to describe these larger creations. The sizes concerned are principally $7\frac{1}{4}$ and $9\frac{1}{2}$ inches between the rails. Many lines exist, especially in Britain and the United States, although there is an unfortunate schism as regards the smaller of the two sizes in the United States. In the west $7\frac{1}{2}$-inch gauge is used while in the east $7\frac{1}{4}$-inch is the norm. Both private and club-owned lines exist, the latter are particularly prominent in North America.

The origins of these sizes lie with the famous British model firm Bassett-Lowke Ltd of Northampton and with the famous designer Henry Greenly, who chose the gauges to go with engineering draftsmans' scales of $1\frac{1}{2}$ and 2 inches to the foot. The $7\frac{1}{4}$- and $7\frac{1}{2}$-inch gauge is now much used to accommodate models of narrow-gauge locomotives. With such narrow-gauge locomotives of greater overall width in relation to the gauge, one can go a step further still and sit not just *on* but also *in* the locomotive. This occurs when the inside width of the tender exceeds 17 inches. Keith Watson of Rossmayne, Western Australia, has pioneered a $7\frac{1}{4}$-inch gauge locomotive wide enough to accommodate two people.

That very first model locomotive, Murdoch's little fire chariot of 1784, seems to have been similar in size to a $7\frac{1}{4}$-inch gauge locomotive although, since there were then no full-size ones, one cannot say that it was a model to some particular scale. So the origins of this size of model railroading are as ancient as possible.

Bassett-Lowke's railroad catalogues issued before World War II always used to include offerings of locomotives and rolling stock in $1\frac{1}{2}$- and 2-inch scales with seductive illustrations. The firm's successors such as David Curwen of Devizes, Severn-Lamb Ltd of Stratford-upon-Avon, Robert Moore of Melton Mowbray, John Milner of Chester, England, and Little Engines of Lonnita, California, have less enticing catalogues but even more seductive products.

In Britain, the smaller of the two sizes has its own flourishing $7\frac{1}{4}$-inch Gauge Society, while all sizes are catered for by the Heywood Society, whose origins are dealt with in Chapter 12. The $9\frac{1}{2}$-inch size has never developed to the extent that its rival has, but remains the province of a few devoted individualists as do S and TT gauges. In fact, $9\frac{1}{2}$-inch gauge has become rather overshadowed by $10\frac{1}{4}$-inch, the 'railway-in-your-park' size, which is also covered in the next chapter.

Below: Early Bassett-Lowke: the $10\frac{1}{4}$-inch line belonging to Mr Franklin at Radwell, Hertfordshire, England. The locomotive is a standard 4-4-2 finished off in North British Railway style. The date is before 1914.

Above: The same 4-4-2 from Radwell, as restored in 1975.

In addition to producing an excellent magazine and also developing a code of practice, the 7¼-inch Gauge Society has a pleasant custom of arranging meets or rallies on members' lines. Vans, caravans and trailers converge on the chosen locality and soon the tracks are busy with the chuffing of steam, as well as the less pleasant noises and smells of internal combustion. An excellent rule is that the feeding and servicing of loco-motives and drivers does not devolve on to the host. Of course such affairs are old hat across the Atlantic, where most live steam clubs offer 7¼- or 7½-inch gauge as well as the smaller sizes, and rallies are a way of life, the great distances involved proving no obstacle.

If you want to build your own line in this size, one question at least is answered for you – whether to go outdoors or indoors. Railroads in as large a gauge as this just cannot be built indoors and, indeed, the average yard is of barely adequate size. The problem is of course our old enemy the turning circle; if the radius is made as sharp as 20 feet, then the type of loco-motive which can be run are limited to small industrial locomotives. A 35-foot radius curve, on the other hand, can accommodate most railroad machinery, but then, not everyone has the space for this.

This brings us to an important point – the important processes of survey, design and setting out have hardly been touched upon, although they are relevant to a small degree in all sizes and are quite significant in the sizes dealt with in the last two chapters. Very often when designing rail grades in miniature one can dis-pense with the need for a survey by using the site as a sort of full-size drawing board, setting out straights and curves by trial and error.

The easy way to set out a curve is to place a temporary

Jack Howey's first pre-1914 passenger-hauling railroad – a 10¼-inch gauge line using another Bassett-Lowke 4-4-2, this time in Great Northern style. Howey went on to build the famous Romney, Hythe & Dymchurch Railway.

Above: A 15-inch gauge steam breakdown crane by EH Jeynes makes a lift at an open day on the Ravenglass and Eskdale Railway. The crane can also travel, slew or luff by steam power.

Left: Heavy civil engineering on another private passenger-hauling railroad, at a secret location in Kent, England.

metal bar or stake in the position where the center might be expected to be located, then try out the curve by swinging a tape measure about the center, holding it at the mark corresponding to the radius proposed. A few attempts gets one very close to the optimum – or proves that the scheme will not work.

If there is an obstruction which prevents the center position being used in this way – for example, it might happen to be inside the house – possible curves can almost as easily be tried by using offsets as a means of curve-ranging. Elementary geometry shows us that if you have two points which are on a curve, a third one can be found by siting the line between the other two and offsetting from it a certain distance. If the three points are at equal intervals L, then the amount to be offset is $\frac{L^2}{R}$ where R is the radius. For a 36-foot radius,

with siting points at 6-foot intervals, the offset is 1 foot. For easy siting, a modest investment in four surveyor's striped poles (banderoles) is worthwhile; each new point is successively set out from the two previous ones.

Two other points about curves are worth noting. First, the only important piece of information one needs to know about a major railroad mystery called a transition curve is that straights should be set out a few inches *outside* the curve to which they are nominally tangential. Second, the provision of banking, cant or super-elevation on miniature railroad curves is much more likely to be a menace than a boon, so limit it to as small a figure as you can bear to – $\frac{1}{4}$ of an inch is ample.

Levels are extremely important when designing a railroad grade, as explained by Sir Arthur Heywood. The weight which can be hauled by a locomotive is drastically reduced as the gradient increases, as follows:

   On a level gradient a locomotive can haul 10 times
   its own weight
   On a 1 in 50 gradient a locomotive can haul 4
   times its own weight
   On a 1 in 25 gradient a locomotive can haul 2
   times its own weight
   On a 1 in 12 gradient a locomotive can haul 1
   times its own weight

Moreover, the eye is easily deceived when assessing levels and nasty surprises await people who rely simply on observation in this respect. Obviously a surveyor's level and staff is ideal but although such equipment can easily be borrowed or hired, training and experience is needed to use them effectively. However, a simple device consisting of a length of plastic tube (or two lengths connected by the garden hose) partly filled with water can be used instead. Since in these conditions the water level at either end will be the same, the relationship between the level of any two points around the site can easily be found, using the water level in the pipe as a datum – provided the pipe is long enough. Remember, gradients steeper than 2–5 percent or 1 in 40 tend to cause problems.

Currently, in this size there is a problem as regards the supply of rail. In most ways steel is the best (and also the correct) material to use but a suitable section is not produced. One is left with three choices; to use aluminum rail which is available but looks wrong, either new or oxidized when weathered; to use steel rail of the smallest commercial size which looks wrong because it is too big or to use some other steel section such as channel or bar – this looks wrong because it is the wrong shape. Examples of all three types of rail can be found where miniature plate laying is practiced.

Above: The 7¼-inch gauge meet: narrow-gauge locomotives 'on shed' at the roundhouse of Doctor Brian Rogers' Porters Hill Railway, near Worcester, England.

Far left: A 7¼-inch gauge locomotive that can be sat in: Jim Haylock's enchanting Heywood-style 0-4-2T *Talos* by Roger Marsh.

Left: A delightful 7¼-inch gauge Decauville type 0-4-0T by Georges Auclair of Beauchamp, France.

Left: The author's 7¼-inch gauge 4-8-2 + 2-8-4 oil-fired Beyer-Garratt *Mount Kilimanjaro* on its home line. The locomotive is 19 feet 6 inches long and weighs nearly two tons.

Right: *Mount Kilimanjaro* in distinguished company at the opening of the National Railway Museum by the Duke of Edinburgh at York in September 1975. Note the full-size model of 'Locomotion' in steam in the background.

Left: At the Peco Modelrama, near Seaton, Devon, England, which includes model railroads in many sizes, starting at N gauge, the largest is this 7¼-inch gauge Beer Heights Railway. The train is shown here passing amid the manicured surroundings of this model factory.

All these weighty matters should serve to remind you that passenger-hauling railroads are in a different league to the others. Very often, in order to achieve an acceptable combination of minimum grade and curvature, substantial earthworks are needed; one even has to consider bringing in engineering plant such as excavators, bulldozers and dumpers. Of course, manual labor can suffice and even a 7¼-inch gauge line is excellent at transporting spoil in bulk – a vivid illustration of the excellence of the railroad for bulk transportation.

When live passengers are carried in cars so small a size, the weights tend to be quite out of proportion (in fact the scale axle load can be the equivalent of 160 tons!) and accordingly scale ⅛ of full-size permanent way is not often found. One man who has developed such material and who intends to use it is EC Martin of Thame, Buckinghamshire, England, on his Garden & Woodland Railway layout which is designed to keep alive the memory of the legendary Great Western Railway. In the past, a Mr Darroch of Crewe made a 9½-inch line with 'exact' scale model permanent way.

For passenger-carrying garden railroads, I advocate the oversize but proper steel rail (in fact, the standard British 'Mines' 14 pounds-per-yard section) and readers must judge for themselves from the illustrations whether the appearance is satisfactory. The Denver and Rio Grande Western narrow gauge tended toward grass-grown sheep-mown permanent way and where this occurs on the Croesor Junction & Pacific Railway the high rail is not apparent. One advantage is that small streams can be bridged by the rail alone. Another is that the Australian Jarrah sleepers can accordingly be widely spaced and substantial, with real ballast to support real, rather than model, loads. Squareheaded screws with washers are used as fastenings and the whole structure not only gives very good running but is also largely maintenance free.

For cases where the passenger carrying element is very modest, scale aluminum permanent way does very well, but it is advisable to have at least two carrying axles under each adult body. Scale nonpassenger-carrying rolling stock appears to complement scale model locomotives in this size – the eye seems to be able to ignore the giant driver sitting on the tender, his feet on the cab floor but knees well above the cab roof.

One line where 1½ inches to 1 foot scale model trains are run is The Spinney Railway at Runfold near Farnham, England. The owner has installed fully-interlocked mechanical signalling, as described in Chapter 8, on the many junctions of his railroad. London & North Western Railway signal practice is followed.

GREAT WESTERN

Left: The 9½-inch gauge railroad built by Mr Darroch, Assistant Works Manager of the Crewe Works of the old London & North Western Railway. Note the superb effect of manicured permanent way laid with material exactly to scale.

Next page: This Denver & Rio Grande 7¼-inch K-36 class 2-8-2 locomotive is a product of the Curwen Locomotive Works – the only one in the world with a thatched roof.

Scale model trains running on scale model track are common in North America. For example, Santa Barbara, California, is the locale of one of the most extensive 7½-inch gauge layouts ever constructed. Seymour Johnson's Goleta Valley Railway has 8000 feet of track, a proper roundhouse with 12 stalls, a seven-track station and some spectacular trestle bridges. There are estimated to be over 35 miles of 7¼- and 7½-inch track active in the United States.

Little has been said about locomotive building in this size, and that is perhaps because there is little to add. Even batch-production is very rare, although Roger Marsh of Hinckley, Leicestershire, England, has recently produced a batch of six of his enchanting Tinkerbell locomotives. These are models of themselves in 12 inches to 1 foot scale, for the prototype was designed as a 7¼-inch gauge steam-haulage unit in its own right.

Smaller 7¼- and 7½-inch gauge locomotives can be built in the average home workshop – indeed, some are specifically designed for this – but larger ones are usually wholly or partly built by the specialists previously mentioned. Most of the work is of the one-off kind and accordingly far from cheap. The spectrum of weight and size in garden railroad power ranges from 0-4-0 tank locomotives weighing, say, 70 pounds and measuring 2 feet in length, to 4-8-2 + 2-8-4 Beyer-Garratts weighing 3800 pounds and 20 feet long. Even nonarticulated locomotives can be found – inevitably from that overmodelled narrow-gauge line, the Denver & Rio Grande Western Railroad – weighing up to 1700 pounds and measuring up to 15 feet long.

While most railways and railroads in this so-called garden size are laid to 7¼- or 7½-inch gauge, the neglected and therefore now rare 9½-inch size is kept alive by a few notable examples both in Britain and elsewhere. John Hall-Craggs has a circular layout in his garden at Brightwalton near Newbury. He also acts as an archivist for 9- and 9½-inch gauge and has records of most lines which ever existed. In 9-inch gauge one notes a long-lived 40-year-old system at a secret location in Kent some distance inland from the famous White Cliffs of Dover. The Torry Hill Railway boasts a curved tunnel, a nice sliding fit for the human frame and long enough so that when in the middle one cannot see daylight at either end. The length of run from terminus to terminus is a fantastic 1¾ miles and the motive power represents famous examples from the head end of the great trains from the steam age in England.

There is also a fine South African 9½-inch example at Kloof near Durban, which has models of the very fine local Cape-gauge locomotives, including a superb GF class 2-6-2 + 2-6-2 Beyer-Garratt, built by Derek Colyer of Durban. The last word on garden railroads, however, remains with 9½-inch gauge, because the oldest one still running is the 54-year-old Downs School Railway at Colwall, England.

Above: Correct scale in 7¼-inch gauge: Ted Martin's reincarnation of the Great Western Railway at Thame, England.

Left: A 7¼-inch gauge diamond-stacked old-timer 2-8-0 of the Denver & Rio Grande Railroad by Milner Engineering of Chester.

Right: The oldest 9½-inch gauge railroad still in existence, the Downs School at Colwall, Herefordshire, England. A model North British Railway 0-4-0 emerges from the tunnel under the road.

12 Railroads in the Park

In going yet larger in this world of model railroads, we find that one factor obtrudes into everything that is done. This, of course, is money and by rights this chapter should be devoted to things like profit and loss accounts, cash flow projections, advertising budgets and all the other financial aspects of running a business.

In all sizes from Z upward the cost of building and equipping the line is very significant to the owner, but somewhere about the $10\frac{1}{4}$-inch gauge size, the cost of running starts to worry him. One solution is to invite people in and ask them to share the cost in return for rides. So $10\frac{1}{4}$-, 12-, and 15-inch gauge railroads tend to occur in the grounds of zoos, stately homes, municipal parks, sites by the sea and similar places. There are a large number spread across the world. Many, of course, are unremarkable childrens trains, equipped as cheaply (and nastily) as possible to make money, and these have no place in this book. On the other hand there is certainly a place for those who put some degree of authenticity first and the regrettable necessity of making enough money to be authentic second. In some cases this has also turned out to be sound business sense for what might generically be termed park railroads.

The man who is generally regarded as the father of 'big little' railroads is Sir Arthur Percival Heywood, baronet, of Duffield Bank, Derby, England. His name has already been mentioned in the last chapter and will occur again in the next, for his work does not fall nicely into present-day categorization. In fact he advocated miniature railroads for hauling the freight associated with agriculture as well as in stately homes. Like George Stephenson's 4-foot $8\frac{1}{2}$-inch, Heywood's 15-inch gauge can be found all over the world, even in metric countries and his book *Minimum Gauge Railways* gave chapter and verse to prove that little steam railroads could be worthwhile for small flows of traffic.

Heywood's line at Duffield Bank was an exquisite toy and boasted 1 in 12 gradients, amazing 25-foot radius curves (15 feet in sidings!) round which eight-coupled locomotives worked. He had both a dining car and a sleeping car, equipped mainly with the sort of fixtures

Right: Sir Arthur Percival Heywood's 15-inch gauge Duffield Bank Railway. View of Tennis Ground Station with 0-4-0T *Effie* (near left) and 0-6-0T *Ella* (far right).

Below: A sleeping car for a 15-inch gauge park railroad! The young Heywoods and their guests used it when the house at Duffield Bank was full. Occasionally an all-night nonstop service was operated.

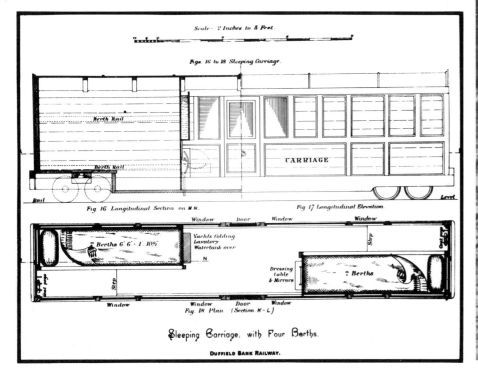

Above left: Double-shotted varnish on the double 15-inch gauge track of the Dresden Pioneer Railway in East Germany. Two 4-6-2s by Krauss of Munich.

Left: At the main station of the 7¼-inch gauge Hilton Valley Railway, in Shropshire, England, a Heywood-style 0-4-2T *Gurkha* by Roger Marsh awaits departure. Neil Simkins, another well-known builder of small steam locomotives, is at the throttle.

Above: Munich, Germany: noble 15-inch gauge 4-6-2 supplied by Krauss & Co for an exhibition park. The locomotive was designed by Roland Martens in close collaboration with Henry Greenly.

and fittings used on pleasure yachts. The diner was used for picnics and the sleeper as overflow accommodation for younger guests during house parties. Heywood's original thinking and successful ideas permeated all the other aspects of his railroad, which was a model one in both senses of the word. Heywood's one customer was the Duke of Westminster and the railroad which connected Eaton Hall, near Chester, with the Great Western Railway at Balderton Station, four miles away, was a model of its kind and lasted until 1950. Freight was its normal business, but passengers included, among many crowned heads, such commoners as Winston Churchill and David Lloyd George. It is a pleasure to write of a rumor that the present Duke intends a two-mile resurrection, with 12-inches to 1 foot scale replica Heywood equipment, plus some original, to carry tourists who visit the estate.

The scene now shifts to New York where, from 1894 onward, in their office on Broadway, the four brothers

Cagney sold miniature 4-4-0 locomotives of four different gauges – 22-, 18-, 15-, and 12-inch – to amusement parks and fairgrounds for the haulage of joyriding passengers. The locomotives were slightly crude representations of the famous New York Central RR No 119 credited slightly dubiously with a world speed record of 112mph in 1893. Two firms built the locomotives for the Cagneys – The McGarigle Machine Co of Niagara Falls, owned by their uncle, and the Herschell Spillman Co of North Tonawanda, New York State – and several hundreds were made.

After a period of eclipse in the 1920s during which Federal Regulations insisted on a second man (for whom there was no room) on the footplate of even a miniature steam locomotive, Cagney-style operations are again increasing. A firm called Crown Metal Products of Wyano, Pennsylvania, offers simple 4-4-0s in 15-, 24-, and 36-inch gauges at surprisingly modest prices, suitable for the kinds of lines described here.

Right: Baroda, India: a miniature railroad in the public park, once the Royal Palace grounds. The locomotive is a London & North Eastern Railway-style 4-6-2 in 10¼-inch gauge by Charles Bullock of Farnborough, England, which once ran on the Surrey Border & Camberley Railway.

Left: Again at Castledare, the same massive locomotive enters the station with a trainload of passengers. The world record for haulage of 125 passengers in one train on the 7¼-inch gauge is claimed by this engine and this railroad.

Above: At Castledare a 2¼-inch scale model of a Western Australian Government Railways P-class 4-8-2 comes 'off shed' on this Antipodean 7¼-inch gauge line.

Two famous names now again appear on the scene – Wenman Joseph Bassett-Lowke and Henry Greenly, who in 1904 became respectively Managing Director and Engineer of Miniature Railways (Great Britain) Ltd, which was intended not only to build and equip miniature railroads but also to run them. *Little Giant* of 1905 was the precursor of 14 handsome 15-inch gauge 4-4-2s of scale appearance but following no particular prototype, which went to many zoo, park and exhibition railroads all over Britain. One even went to the King of Siam and others worked in Budapest, Brussels, Nancy (France), Oslo and Geneva. There is a possibility of a treasure trove, for four remain untraced to this day.

Commercial passenger operations of this type on 10¼-inch gauge began around the same date, when an 0-4-4 tank locomotive designed by Henry Greenly took the rails at Bricket Wood, Hertfordshire, England, and although slower to start has now become – in Britain, anyway – the favorite size for these 'park' railroads. It can now be found as far afield as Baroda, India, and Vancouver, Canada.

Charles Bullock developed this size between the wars and after 1945 David Curwen set up what was almost a production line for very massive and simple 10¼-inch 4-4-2s and 4-6-2s. Curwen has been called the Henry Ford of small locomotive building, though others feel that Count Bugatti – who asked a customer to lunch

Above: A well-equipped narrow-gauge 4-6-0T *Karalee* on the Castledare Miniature Railway. Note the purpose-made separate driving truck, turbo-generator to feed the headlight and scale 'chopper' coupling.

to be looked over before selling him a car – was a closer parallel among the motor men. This $2\frac{1}{4}$ inches to 1 foot scale was a very good size as, for example, normal commercial steam fittings could be used – in both larger and smaller sizes it is usually necessary to use specialist ones – while a locomotive built to this scale was comfortably wide enough for the driver.

A gauge of $10\frac{1}{4}$ inches provides the basis for what must be considered a candidate for the world's summit among any model and miniature locomotives ever built. This is the 'Berkshire' 2-8-4 of the Nickel Plate Road in the United States which works on the Stapleford Miniature Railway, in the grounds of Stapleford Park, near Melton Mowbray, England. The locomotive not only duplicates almost every nut and bolt of its fairly complex prototype, but one also finds that most of its accessories actually work. For example, are there any other model locomotives with a working automatic stoker? The presence of duplicate automatic duplex cross compound air pumps is only just less remarkable, as is a *pair* of working turbogenerators. Provision for a full-size driver is ingeniously unobtrusive and the performance is excellent. Credit for design and build-

ing goes to Richard Coleby, Neil Simkins, Bob Moore and David Vere. Credit for the concept, plus the courage to go ahead, goes to the owner, The Honorable John Gretton. The line on which the Berkshire runs is equally outstanding, with $1\frac{3}{4}$ miles of track, exciting bridges, tunnels and more than all the usual fixtures.

Standardization is less important in these sizes from the point of view of first cost, although disposal or redeployment is much easier if a line is laid to one of the standard gauges. Even so, individualists implement their own ideas. One example is the late E Carrington Eddy's marvellous Pinconning & Blind River Railroad in the backwoods near Fairview, Michigan, America. This is made to 16-inch gauge and includes – as one might expect on a lumberman's line – rather exciting timber trestle bridges and passovers.

This brings us to two important points concerning miniature model railroads. First, they need to have thrills (of a safe kind) on a miniature railroad circuit. A trestle bridge provides excitement, as does a tunnel, such as the one on the Stapleford Park Railway. The second point is rather a sad one. This size of railroad is usually an intensely personal affair and when the

founder of the line dies his railroad is liable to decline. Many unfortunate cases can be cited, but hopefully the line at Fairview will not be one of them.

Narrow-gauge versions of the park railroad are now high fashion and it is also worth noting the continued existence of a broad-gauge line at Littlehampton, England. Two of Charles Bullock's $10\frac{1}{4}$-inch gauge 4-6-2s were altered, either during construction or afterward, to 12-inch gauge, the equivalent of 5 feet 4 inches in full-size measure.

One of the oldest of the narrow-gauge style lines is the 15-inch gauge Redwood & Pacific Railroad at Tilden Park, in the hills above Berkeley, San Francisco. The scale of 5 inches to 1 foot is a large one, but the little 2-4-2 which does the honors would be a very small machine in full size. An advantage of the large scale is that the cars can be actual models of real ones and still be adapted to carry full-size passengers. Also made to this size, but with larger 2-8-0 and 2-6-2 locomotives based on the Denver & Rio Grande Western RR, are trains in Scottsdale, a suburb of Phoenix, Arizona. It has the entirely appropriate title of Paradise & Pacific Railroad.

The railroad which possibly offered the most excitement was called the Hilton Valley Railway. It was the brainchild of the late Michael Lloyd, a Midlands Industrialist. It was laid to $7\frac{1}{4}$-inch gauge but the relatively small capacity of the trains did not matter because of their frequency. Safety was ensured by a token system based on full-size signalling regulations, whereby a driver had to be in possession of a physical token of authority to be on each single-line section. These tokens had to be respectively picked up and set down at each end of each section each time; drinks all round afterward if a driver forgot one. The system has recently moved and now runs in the grounds of Weston House, near Telford, Shropshire, England.

Another $7\frac{1}{4}$-inch gauge line, but with trains that are (in the notation applied to smaller sizes) either 15n2 or $10\frac{1}{4}$n$3\frac{1}{2}$ is the Castledare Miniature Railway of Western Australia. Of course, a gauge of $3\frac{1}{2}$ feet is standard in that part of the world, 4 feet $8\frac{1}{2}$ inches being just a tentacle of the Trans-Australian Railway, so the scale-gauge combination suits models of local motive power. An engineer called Keith Watson is the prime mover in this project, which is full of thrills such as truss girder

Two locomotives by David Curwen on the 10¼-inch gauge Audley End Miniature Railway. To the left is a Great Northern 4-4-2, based on an enlargement of the 3½-inch gauge 'Maisie' design by LBSC of the Model Engineer. On the right is a standard American-type 4-4-2.

bridges, tunnels and sharply curved convolutions. The line is situated in the grounds of a home for orphaned and deprived children and the setup nicely illustrates an ideal benefits-all-round system. The orphanage raises money, the children have an absorbing (and attractively messy) activity on their doorstep, the local live-steamers have a superb railroad on which to practice their hobby and local families have a convenient and pleasant park in which to spend a free day. The Castledare railroad is a great success, a measure of which is its claim to the record for the largest number of passengers ever carried on a single $7^1/_4$- or $7^1/_2$-inch gauge train. This is 125, so overtaking the previous record of 117 plus one dog held by the Hilton Valley Railroad. Locomotives concerned were, respectively, models of a Western Australian Government Railways' 4-8-2 and the East African Railways Beyer-Garratt locomotive *Mount Kilimanjaro*. A return match is awaited when more rolling stock is available.

Readers will observe that this chapter contains less how-to-do-it material than the others. One reason is that methods and techniques differ very little – apart from things like fare collection – from those of Chapter 11. The other reason is that the lines described are there for anyone to enjoy for the price of a ticket. Some part can be played with too, in so far as some managements welcome volunteer help, if reliable and willing and especially, of course, if skilled as well.

Volunteer work is really only appropriate for railroads that are commercial in a limited sense, that is,

that they charge enough just to clear their running expenses. Very often they confine their operations to weekends and holidays and there is no real prospect of earning any interest on capital which lies idle for 300 days out of 365. If one glances around the railroads of the world from $1/_4$-inch (Z) gauge to 5-foot 6-inches, the number that are a real commercial success can almost be counted on the fingers of one hand. Union Pacific is one and Sante Fe another, the Benguela Railway in Angola was a third until the communists took over, and then there is the Forest Railway of Liskeard, Cornwall, England. The story of the Forest Railway illustrates many points in connection with success in the small railroad field.

John Southern was a farmer in Cornwall. His interest in railroads centered on a 5-inch gauge live-steam railroad in his garden when, almost by chance, he acquired a very fine London, Midland & Scottish Railway 4-6-2 *Duchess of Montrose* in $7^1/_4$-inch gauge. The 5-inch gauge was then abandoned and a circuit laid out for the larger size. Soon, in his own words, 'people started looking longingly over the fence and I began to invite them in.'

As a farmer he was accustomed to regard land, and in particular the land the railroad was laid on, as an asset and a challenge. Therefore, before long he started charging for admission. People on vacation wanting a bit of a change from the bucket-and-spade routine of the beaches soon swamped the capacity of this garden railroad.

Above: Forest Railroad Park: *William Jeffers* ready to go.

Right: Forest Railroad Park: Union Pacific 'Big Boy' 4-8-8-4 *William Jeffers* crosses a flyover trestle bridge near the summit of the Sherman Hill.

Around this time David Curwen showed Southern a narrow-gauge locomotive which was taking shape in his workshop near Devizes. It was from the Denver & Rio Grande Western again! The advantages of changing to narrow gauge are vividly illustrated by the figures below.

Locomotive	LMS Duchess	D & RGW K-36
Wheel arrangement	4-6-2	2-8-2
Gauge	7¼ inches	7¼ inches
Scale	⅛	½
Cylinder size	2½-inch bore by 3½-inch stroke	4-inch bore by 5-inch stroke
Boiler diameter	8 inches	14 inches
Weight (less tender)	550 pounds	1800 pounds

The Duchess was disposed of and the K-36 was acquired plus a Curwen-built internal-combustion machine. Southern obtained other engines, an ultra-simple diamond-stacker narrow-gauge 0-6-0 and a superb Union Pacific '800' class 4-8-4, which was built 'overscale' – rather in the manner of the OO-gauge locomotives running on 16.5mm rather than the true 18.83mm gauge – to match the K-36 2-8-2.

Additional convolutions with exciting tunnels and earthworks were added to the circuit, a cafe, shop and car park were built, picnic grounds and a plantation were laid out – hence the name Forest Railway – and, most crucial of all, the railroad replaced farming as the source of the family's income.

The theme of the layout was now the Railroading of the American West and to emphasize this, features were named after famous locations such as Lost Souls Canyon, Toltec Tunnel, Windy Point, Chattanooga and so on. All this added to the success of the line, which being now hidden from the road was able to take money from spectators as well as riders. Full multiaspect electric signalling permitted the safe working of a frequent service and up to four trains running at once provides great excitement.

In 1979 a second circuit was opened, taking the place of the old pig houses, the theme of this being the famous Sherman Hill out of Cheyenne on the Union Pacific Railroad. To work the new line there was the existing UP 4-8-4 and, in addition, Severn-Lamb of Stratford-on-Avon delivered an amazing 'Big Boy' 4-8-8-4 as well as a 'Centennial' diesel locomotive. Denver & Rio Grande RR motive power (augmented by a second 2-8-2) remains on the original circuit. There are very few other contenders for the title of premier park railroad than the one now called the Forest Railroad.

Above: Forest Railroad Park: Union Pacific FEF 1 4-8-4 No 818 *Queen of Wyoming* hauls a trainload of passengers on the opening day of the Sherman Hill extension in April 1979.

Above: The magnificent ¼-inch scale 10¼-inch gauge Berkshire 2-8-4 based on the famous class of locomotive from the Nickel Plate Road, which runs on the Stapleford Park Railway.

Right: A handsome narrow-gauge 2-6-4T of the much mourned Manifold Valley Light Railway. The model runs on a 10¼-inch gauge line at Rudyard Lake, Staffordshire.

13　Passenger-hauling Model Railroads

At the absolute top of the model railroad tree come the lines which really go places. By this is meant those that are miniature in form but carry out full-size functions, that is, they provide transport between two distinct locations, which we will arbitrarily specify to be more than two miles apart. They are so few in number that all the ones have ever existed can receive a mention. It may surprise you to learn that among these there are some which have (or had) actual Statutory Authority – sometimes called a Charter or Franchise – to obtain land compulsorily, as well as to exist thereafter for ever. History was made in 1925 when Captain Jack Howey applied to the British parliament for a Light Railway Order to build a 15-inch gauge miniature line across Romney Marsh, connecting the ancient British south-coast harbor towns of Romney and Hythe.

So Romney Marsh added to its more ancient claims to fame the fact that it is now the site of what is without doubt the largest model railroad in the world (some 300,000 people visit it each year), called the Romney Hythe & Dymchurch Railway. One might almost say that the world's railroads divide into three, that is full size, model and the RH&DR.

Howey had spent those fat Edwardian years before World War I setting up a private miniature line in his park at Staughton Manor, Warwickshire. During the war years which followed he had leisure to contemplate the future from behind the barbed wire of a prisoner-of-war camp. He came back with the amazing and certainly original idea of constructing several miles of model railroad with the purpose of providing a public service over a tract of hitherto railroadless countryside.

Above: Romney, Hythe & Dymchurch Railway 0-4-0: *The Bug* negotiates an open level crossing, newly equipped with automatically controlled road-traffic signals.

Fortunately he owned a sufficiently large tract of the city of Melbourne, Australia, for money not to be a problem. The result was that by 1930 13 real and 40 scale miles of (15-inch gauge) double-track main line, on which nine 4-6-2 and 4-8-2 locomotives hauled (and haul) loads of pleasure-seekers, which in the past have included Prince Charles, Queen Elizabeth II and her father, then Duke of York.

Some 200 pupils of New Romney School are in fact the only nonpleasure customers, travelling morning and evening during the school term. The sight of a crowd of 200 scale-model commuters treading New Romney station in indeed worth seeing. Steam traction is used, apart from the use of a tractor for works trains. All the original and, indeed, all subsequently acquired steam locomotives are currently in use on the line and what

railroads, real or model, after more than 50 years can boast of that?

To design and build the RH&DR, Howey engaged Henry Greenly who applied his experience to adjusting the design of the most famous locomotives of the day – the London & North Eastern Flying Scotsman 4-6-2s – so that a 1/3-scale model could run on track which was only just over 1/4 of scale width. Of the five 4-6-2s two, (*Typhoon* and *Hurricane*), even had the third inside cylinder as fitted to the full-size machines. In later years this complication was found not to be worthwhile and the inside motion was removed, so making, after consequent changes, the two locomotives concerned similar to the original three (*Green Goddess, Southern Maid* and *Northern Chief*). Some freight traffic was handled and for this some might-have-been LNER 4-8-2s (*Samson*

Above: Romney, Hythe & Dymchurch Railway: the famous daily school train leaves New Romney during the wintry weather of January 1979.

Next page: Pinconning & Blind River Railroad: 4-6-2 No 5661 at the water tank on this 16-inch gauge line at Fairview, Michigan, USA.

Below: Romney, Hythe & Dymchurch Railway: 4-8-2 *Hercules* rolls into Dymchurch Station on the double-track main line.

Next page: Ravenglass & Eskdale Railway: 0-8-2 *River Irt* brings a train down the dale.

FOR ALL TYPES OF PROPERT
TO BE LET OR SOLD
FURNISHED HOLIDAY BUNGAL

APPLY

TINSLEY & CLINC

ESTATE AGENTS

| COAST DRIVE GREATSTONE NEW ROMNEY 3193 | HIGH ST NEW ROMNEY NEW ROMNEY 3194 | HIGH ST DYMCHU DYMCHU 212 |

Above: Ravenglass & Eskdale Railway: Dalegarth Station with 2-8-2 *River Mite* ready to depart.

Left: Romney, Hythe & Dymchurch Railway: signalman's view of train arriving at Hythe.

and *Hercules)* were used as prototypes. All these locomotives were constructed by Davey Paxman & Co, of Colchester, Essex.

Later, two Canadian Pacific-style 4-6-2s, *Winston Churchill* and *Dr Syn*, were constructed partly at New Romney and, as recently as 1976, a German 4-6-2 *(Black Prince)* by Krupp of Essen was acquired secondhand from a park railroad in Cologne. Lastly, there is *The Bug*, an 0-4-0 from Krauss of Germany, supplied for the construction of the line, and subsequently sold. Her recovery from the bottom of a scrapheap in Northern Ireland and subsequent rebuilding is a book in itself. The whole locomotive fleet is beautifully consistent in scale and a most precious and remarkable reminder of all that was best in main-line steam operation.

Greenly was also responsible for every detail of the line from station toilets to the tower clock, perhaps his only serious mistake in all this was the use of shingle for ballast. Shingle is formed of round stones that entirely fail to interlock as they should and so do not do their job of supporting the track. Sharp stones are needed for ballast if permanent way is to live up, even temporarily, to its name. Howey had been a motor racing driver and stories of his speed exploits have probably lost rather than gained in the telling. One summer's day he closed the line so that he and his friend, Sir Henry Seagreave, could race locomotives on the double track. Hopefully they had the open level crossings specially guarded!

Recent developments have included renewal of many coaches, new buildings at Hythe and New Romney, as well as an elegant buffet car on some trains. These serve both alcoholic and nonalcoholic drinks at all times, for licensing laws do not apply on statutory railroads in Britain.

Left: Réseau Guerlédan: the Darjeeling-Himalayan 0-4-0.

Above: Romney, Hythe & Dymchurch Railway: 4-6-2 *Hurricane* at The Pilot halt on special train for a British Railways' staff outing.

Below: Riverside & Great Northern Railroad: 4-4-2 locomotive running round at terminus. Note the handsome clerestory roof cars.

Nowadays a model railroad of this caliber is beyond the means of a single person and, in fact, 200 or so shareholders have succeeded Jack Howey in ownership of the line (you could own your share – why not apply to the company at The Railway Station at New Romney, Kent, England) which still has no near rival as the 'biggest little railroad in the world.'

Henry Greenly was recommended to Howey as his engineer for the line on the grounds of his experience (with Bassett-Lowke and others) in taking over in 1915 a derelict 6-mile narrow-gauge mineral railroad in the Lake District, England, called the Ravenglass & Eskdale Railway. It was then converted on a shoestring budget and without statutory authority to a 15-inch gauge miniature line. This is still a wonderful ride and over the years its equipment has been much improved, holding

its place as Number Two among the world's model railroads. The Ravenglass & Eskdale in its turn owed much both in concept and in actual equipment to the Bassett-Lowke park lines described in the previous chapter, but even so, Greenly and others learned the hard way that 'scale,' that is, $\frac{1}{4}$-size equipment, was not robust enough to do the job on such a long heavily graded 15-inch gauge line.

It also owes much to the work of Sir Arthur Heywood because after his death in 1916 most of the equipment from the Duffield Bank Railway came to Ravenglass, where they formed a remarkable contrast to the Bassett-Lowke $\frac{1}{4}$-scale models already there. To some extent the same is true today with Heywood's 0-8-0T *Muriel*, now rebuilt as 0-8-2 *River Irt*, contrasting with Greenly's $\frac{1}{3}$-scale 2-8-2 *River Esk* and new narrow-gauge style

2-6-2 *Northern Rock* rather overshadowing the 15-year-old main-line style 2-8-2 *River Mite*. From the earliest days internal combustion traction was a feature and this has not changed either. In one matter the R&ER is not in any way Number Two. This is as regards its scenery, which stands comparison with any in the world.

For one brief year of glory, in the same year that the R&ER took its first tentative steps as a miniature railroad, the San Francisco area resounded to the exhaust music of three lovely ⅓-scale 4-6-2s of most authentic design. They ran on a 2-mile double-track railroad of 19-inch gauge which served the grounds of the Panama Pacific Exposition. This was held in San Francisco from January–November 1915 to celebrate the opening of the Panama Canal. A wealthy young man called Louis MacDermot was responsible, but excessive financial

Top: Caligosta Steam Railroad: 4-6-2 built by Louis MacDermot in 1915 still in use in 1978.

Above: Romney, Hythe & Dymchurch Railway: German style 4-6-2 by Krupp of Essen leaving New Romney for Dungeness.

Left: Romney, Hythe & Dymchurch Railway: American-type 4-6-2 *Winston Churchill* on Hythe to New Romney train.

Above: Chemin de Fer de la Loge des Gardes, Roanne, France, half-size 28-inch gauge model 'Wild West' American 4-4-0 No 1.

Below: Réseau Guerlédan: *Galloping Goose* railcar used for works trains.

loss seems to have cured him of such rash enterprise and nothing was heard afterward of any permanent location for his equipment, which was as fine as any which has ever been produced.

The three Pacifics, plus another which had been built but never used, as well as an 0-6-0T which was used for construction work were stored away. After MacDermot's death in 1948 the locomotives passed into the hands of Billy Jones who used the 0-6-0T on his Wildcat RR at Los Gatos, California. The curves of this line were too sharp for the 4-6-2s. This rather sad story has a less sad ending, for after being out of service for over 50 years, two of these handsome locomotives have reappeared on a 2-mile line called the Caligosta Steam Railroad near the town of that name in California, 25 miles north of San Francisco.

Alas, there is no such happy ending for the smallest of all the transport lines. This was the 2-mile Surrey Border & Camberley Railway, laid to $10\frac{1}{4}$-inch gauge. It was a most elaborate affair with double track on part of the main line, a four-platform terminus complete with glass roof at the main station and six or seven locomotives. Train services were run all the year round and self-drive hire of locomotives was offered. The first year's operation in 1938 was a disaster with receipts of £4500 and expenses of £19,000. In 1939 the line was closed – only partly on account of the war – and in time was dismantled and its assets sold. Only £2100 was realized against an expenditure of £16,500. If these figures are multiplied by a factor of 20, one gets the scale of disaster that happened then and could easily happen again today with any ill-considered and over-ambitious scheme. The locomotives (by Charles Bullock) are now scattered, the only one currently believed to be running in public service operates in Baroda, India. This is the 'Flying Scotsman' type 4-6-2 Harvester.

Réseau Guerlédan: the two owners of the line at Mur-de-Bretagne station. The 0-4-0 Darjeeling loco is to the left, Lynton & Barnstaple van to right.

IL EST
DANGEREUX ET
ABSOLUMENT
INTERDIT
DE MARCHER
SUR LES RAILS

Left: Réseau Guerlédan: Lynton & Barnstaple type 2-6-2T *Jubilee*.

Above: Réseau Guerlédan: 2-6-2T *Jubilee* ready to depart from Mur-de-Bretagne.

A line which runs over some distance is especially vulnerable to the fact that large model trains are at least as attractive to look at as to travel in and charging a fee to enter a linear estate a few miles long and a few yards wide is difficult to say the least. A line in a railroad park can get some recompense from the sightseer for the pleasure received.

Wisconsin Dells is a beauty spot in the state of that name where in 1958 the Sandleys, father and son, opened their 4-mile long 15-inch gauge Riverside & Great Northern Railway. This leads out of town on an abandoned Great Northern Railroad grade to Standing Rock, a local vantage point.

In addition to running the little railroad the Sandleys had a business manufacturing equipment for miniature railroads generally. The R&GN was used as a showcase and testing ground for new designs. A neat 4-4-2 is assigned regularly to the train of handsome clerestory-roofed cars. Authenticity is carried beyond the train, the buildings are superb minireplicas of steam-age America, but perhaps the excitement factor is not too prominent on this line.

The abandonment of many branch lines leading to vacation resorts has tempted people to try relaying them as miniature lines. The transfer of statutory powers to an individual for this purpose is complicated legally, as well as being something which British bureaucrats are reluctant to do unless they have considerable confidence in the people to whom the powers are going. This reluctance usually takes the form of very long

delays. A certain successful miniature park railroad operator attempted some years ago to take over the old branch-line grade leading from Axminster to the seaside resort of Lyme Regis in Devon, England. His company borrowed money to buy the necessary rail and equipment, but the delays were such that he eventually had to sell out and abandon the project.

An equally sad story concerns John Ellerton, who is half English and half Welsh, but who has spent a lot of his life in America. He appeared on the miniature railroad scene in Britain in 1977, ordered himself some gems of narrow-gauge locomotives, chose a site in Brittany, France, and cut through Gallic red tape to such effect that in July, 1978 his 4-mile Réseau Guerlédan opened for business. The site was an abandoned section of the Réseau Breton and the terminus at the real station of Mur-de-Bretagne. It was a delightful enterprise. Unfortunately, soon after the second season began in 1979, some well-wishers began making attempts to derail (*sabotage* of course is a French word) loaded passenger trains. As a result, the line has had to close. So local jealousies can have an effect on vulnerable small railroads and completely dissolve the pleasure enjoyed by numbers of fans.

Ellerton is making attempts to find a new site in Britain. All lovers of little railroads wish him luck; perhaps one day he will be able to run his half-size 12-inch gauge, replicas of Welsh Highland, Lynton & Barnstaple, Manifold Valley and Darjeeling Himalayan locomotives in the country where they were built.

14 Future Technology

Model railroading is certainly a mere frill (although a very nice one) on the fabric of civilization. On the other hand, among nations whose people struggle along only a little above subsistence level such as China or India, there is a fairly minimal production of model trains. However, assuming that the Western world manage to keep to some degree the margin they currently have in their standard of living over and above the necessities of life, then model railroads will continue to develop. If one compares the luscious but relatively primitive toy trains available 50 years ago to the detailed scale models on the shelves of any model shop today, and projects it forward another 50 years, what will be available then?

Of course, the pleasure that model railroads provide will hardly have changed or increased in the smallest degree, however sophisticated the hardware becomes. Leaving that aside, the main change will certainly be due to the silicon-chip revolution, leading to greater realism in matters other than shape or form.

Left: Arthur Sherwood, associate professor of biochemistry at the University of Sydney, Australia, prepares his 1:240 scale butane-fired steam locomotive for the road. Here he puts the butane gas burner into the tender. The funnel extension stops condensation blocking the funnel while steam is being raised.

Above: Filling the boiler with one cubic centimeter of water, using a hypodermic syringe.

Above: The shape of things for which there will be no need in the future; the superb control panel for the Bromford and High Peak Railway with individual switches for the control of separate sections and points.

Features which are now just making a tentative appearance will by then be normal. For example, it would be absurd to imagine that any locomotive sold would not have a unique code built into it, so it would only respond to a controller set to that particular loco. So let us in our imagination ask our friendly local hobby-shopkeeper to place something from his wide choice on the rails of his test track. A New York Central *Niagara* perhaps, or maybe the London & North Eastern's record-breaking 4-6-2 *Mallard;* we could have a super electric loco or train of the 2030s or, alternatively, whatever coal-consuming type of motive power is then used for railroading away from the wires.

So, taking hold of the wire-less (literally) controller, one keys in the individual code belonging to the locomotive to be run. Immediately she responds (if steam) with the noises (vibrating airpump, gentle hissing) of such a locomotive at rest. Forward or reverse is then selected and, assuming it is that kind, there is a suitable response in the form of a movement of the valve gear. First, sound the superb chime whistle as per the regulations, then move over the control handle. Both the chuffing and the rumbling, although synthesized, are truly realistic and stand up well against recordings of what is even in 1980 only history. Their loudness also depends on whether the locomotive is pulling hard with a load on a grade or drifting downhill; in addition the chuffing exactly matches the revolutions of the wheels. Also, of course, the sounds emanate from the actual

locomotive. Perhaps it might be tactful to add an adjustable noise-limit switch for operation within earshot of railroading's occasional nonenthusiast. Diesel and electric locomotive noises would be even easier to simulate but surely, even in the 2030s, less inspiring.

Smoke or steam emission, inertia simulation and independence of occasional momentary loss of electrical contact with the rails would be taken for granted. Although, as regards the former, one doubts whether it will ever be made really realistic. For one thing, the transparency of a smoke or steam cloud depends on its actual rather than its scale thickness.

The general sharpness and authenticity of our hypothetical future model locomotive of the year 2030 would strike visitors from the past as being very remarkable, if the rate of progress achieved between 1930 and 1980 is sustained. This would apply to all else on the model railroad, but particularly (one hopes) to operations.

For example, hump-shunting in a 1980s marshalling yard would be excellent fun but with present technology extremely difficult to do with any realism in a model. Technology in the 2030s should make it simple for the model railroad's minicomputer to set and reset the points between 'cuts' or 'rafts' of freight cars. The problem lies in the lack of inertia or rollability of model cars compared with full size, but even here really frictionless bearings and a slight increase of gradient does help. It is common knowledge that those distant

stars which are called dwarfs, contain matter so compressed that a matchbox could contain several tons. It is possible that in 40 years' time such material could be synthesized on earth. If this was the case, by adding a couple of specks to each wheel model railroad cars with scale rollability would become a reality. Using present-day metals it is necessary to have axles of nearly the same diameter as the wheels to achieve the same effect.

Most serving railroadmen hold the hope that the hit-and-miss business of hump-shunting will be an unmourned memory in 50 years' time; perhaps their wishes (partly fulfilled in one or two localities even today) will come true. Even so, the technology of true automatic shunting, with full control of movement, seems likely to be easier to achieve in model form and may well precede its general adoption in full size.

A few ideas for future model railroad delights which come to mind include such things as trains which slip coaches at up to three successive wayside stations; a train ferry floating in real water which can be loaded with sections of a train, made to set off across a model ocean and dock on the other side ready for unloading and remarshalling. A fully operational breakdown crane, complete with slewing, luffing, lifting and propelling action would also be very acceptable. What would a boy from the future think about a model rail-mounted naval gun of 1916 or 1942, complete with elevating and firing mechanisms?

The sort of computer circuits that are suitable for the silicon chip are often referred to as Go/Not Go logic.

Above: An American in France: an Aster gauge-1 live-steam model of the SNCF 'Liberation' Class 141R. The prototype was supplied by North American locomotive builders to replace the wastage of World War II. The model is gas-fired and represents the peak of present-day functional realism. Hopefully such things will become more common in the future.

Left: The search for realism: the simple way to work points is by electro-magnets, which move the blades almost instantaneously. Real points, however, move across slowly; here is an arrangement for HO scale in which a small electric motor reproduces the action more precisely.

Now, for a railroad signalling system, could such a description be bettered? With the coming of the domestic computer the way would be open for comprehensive signalling without tears.

At present, a properly track-circuited layout fully signalled for running in all directions would normally need between eight and 12 relays per turnout, all tediously wired in. By 2030 it should be quite usual – at a cost no higher than normally considered for model railroad control hardware – to program a small computer to do the job. It would transmit its instructions to an army of points and signals, all unwired except for a simple power supply. All incompatibilities would be prevented by the logic of the computer program and, of course, to the people of 2030, computer programming would be as commonplace as reading and writing. Even in 1980 such a system would be feasible, although fairly expensive.

So what might be the limits of future Lilliputian railroads as regards their imitation of the moving scene of the real thing? In Disneyland one can today watch President Lincoln delivering the Gettysburg address with word and gesture, but somehow one doubts whether such animation will ever be applied generally to the little people of a model railroad. Perhaps there might be such stereotyped exceptions as a Central European station-master coming out of his office and saluting when an express goes through his station, or a dummy steam-locomotive crew miming the driving and firing of their iron horse. Such delights were not unknown in the pre-1914 'tin plate' era of model railroad-

ing. Things of this kind could be combined with full visual feedback so that Gulliver 'on shore' could experience the visual and other sensory sensations of being a miniature driver on the actual permanent way of a Lilliputian model railroad!

As regards increasing the range of model railroad hardware as well as what it will do, it does seem unlikely that sizes smaller than Z will develop. This is not because mankind will find the feat impossible – Wakeley did it in 1938 after all – but because the limitations of human eyesight would seem to prevent real enjoyment of the product. On the other hand, one hopes and suspects that a range of big model main-line trains, built say in 2½-inch gauge, will appear to complement the big narrow-gauge ones already on the market.

The use of future technology could point the model-rail man in quite a different direction. One has already observed that just as the handling of sailing boats and the riding of horses have so long survived their practical use as means of transport, no doubt live steam will still continue in favor. It is even possible that the silicon chip and associated developments will allow manufacturers to produce live-steam hardware by automatic machining and robot assembly which will enable those who are not able or prepared to put in or to pay for those 1000 man-hours of skilled work needed, before they can enjoy ultimate model railroad pleasures, the driving of one's own live steam locomotive.

So, 50 years on, the technology of the future will perhaps enable people to enjoy the technology of 50 years back.

15 Guidance for Modellers

At the very highest social standing in the world of model railroads is the concept of doing it in full size. A recent and incomparable opportunity of enjoying such a feat arose with the recent re-enactment of the Rainhill steam locomotive trials, in celebration of the 150th anniversary of the opening of the world's first intercity railroad between Liverpool and Manchester. Full-size replicas of such famous locomotives as *Rocket, Sans Pareil* and *Novelty* were made for the entertainment and edification of the world at large. In charge of this repeat order for motive power of 1830 design was Michael Satow, who had previously built another 12 inches to 1 foot scale model of Stephenson's *Locomotion* for the Stockton and Darlington celebrations five years earlier.

Of course such large-scale operations are out of reach of individuals and the work was the result of many helping hands in the full-size railroad world as well as industry in general. In this respect Michael Satow's project is a lesson to people who model railroads in more modest sizes. Most of those who start out will have friends or acquaintances who dabble to a greater or lesser degree in model trains and this is an excellent starting point when it comes to advice. To widen the circle most important cities have both model railroad and live-steam clubs. Very often they have layouts of a size and complexity that would be impossible for an individual to build and maintain. A friendly welcome to any newcomer who abides by their rules and customs can be relied upon.

Of all the clubs, societies and associations that exist, way out in front stands the National Model Railroad Association of the United States, with 27,000 members living in 60 countries all over the world. The NMRA was founded in 1935 and now looks after its members from toy-train age onward – even beyond the grave with a comprehensive Estate Counselling Program called The End of the Line!

An annual handbook lists all the members, together with a note of the scale to which they work and some indication of whether visitors would be welcome. The arrangement is geographical, by cities, and anyone who joins has therefore a ready means of getting in touch with local fellow-workers who model railroads North American style.

Among many other benefits, the NMRA lays down mandatory standards for wheels, track and clearances which, over the last 40 years, have succeeded in making various manufacturers' products largely compatible one with another. These standards have spread across the Atlantic, largely because European model-train manufacturers have aspirations to enter the world's largest market, which they have done with some success.

NMRA 'Recommended Practice' sheets cover such items as abbreviations, turnout dimensions, rail sizes, and coupler contours. A sample which well illustrates their comprehensive nature is 'RP 11,' on curvature and rolling stock. General information comes in a huge book of 'Data Sheets' – heavier than a volume of *Encyclopaedia Britannica* – covering every imaginable model-railroad subject under the sun.

The hobby is taken very seriously, with what are virtually examination boards to pass members into elite categories – there are ten in all – such as Master Builder Motive Power, Model Railroad Engineer, Chief Dispatcher or Model Railroad Author. When seven of these Achievement Certificates have been won by someone, he qualifies for the top grade Master Model Railroader. Only 67 of these awards have been made to date.

Both national and regional annual conventions are held and the NMRA also keeps in touch with its members via a professional-standard bulletin. Among the helping hands offered are tape-slide clinic packs covering such subjects as painting locos and making scenery. There is nothing quite like the NMRA elsewhere in the world. For example, the much older Model Railway Club (of Britain) remains small and select, maintaining its own club rooms in London complete with workshop and refreshment facilities – but it has fewer members than even the British Region alone of the NMRA. The MRC's most notable contribution to the hobby generally is the organization of the National Model Railway Exhibition held at Easter each year in London. It is a wonderful eye opener for the newcomer to see the enormous scope and range of the model-railroad craft.

Another way in which practitioners of the craft help one another lies in the vast literature of the subject. Too vast, many would say, for it is difficult to find enough storage space, and even if easily accessible storage space is available indexing only by the year of publication means that the particular items required could still be very elusive. One thing that could well have been added to the 'wish list' for the future in the previous chapter would be a data retrieval system, so that by keying in a word or two one could get an immediate sight of the subject matter one wants.

Even so, there is no doubt that the English-language model-railroad periodicals are superb and one is quite spoiled for choice, with six major monthly magazines devoted to the subject. In each of them, and with only a slightly differing emphasis, the material offered divides in the following way; how-to-do-it articles; illustrations of other people's work from which to learn; information concerning the ways of full-size railroads and reviews of new products and books. Last but not least are the advertisements which again might be divided into categories. The first type merely solicit your custom for mail-order, standard mass-produced goods, while the second and more valuable sort tell of some new, unusual or specially interesting item of the advertiser's own manufacture. With a few honorable exceptions one could say that the less conspicuous the advertisement, the more interesting and valuable it is likely to be.

Numerous other journals, of varying size, quality and frequency of issue cover various specialist aspects, particularly the unusual sizes and scales, such as TT, S, O and 1 gauge. Many of them are the voices of various associations, societies and other groups. Model-railroad clubs of purely local interest also usually produce their own newsletters or magazines. The live-steam interest is also well catered for, with one fortnightly, one quarterly and three monthly periodicals, plus many more lightweight publications of a more private kind.

Even these do not end the list; the annual appearance of manufacturers' catalogues must not be forgotten. These vary from magnificent books in full color – quite eclipsing in finery any of the magazines – down to those which consist only of a few handwritten duplicated sheets. But beware, model-railroad catalogues must be regarded as among the most seductive items of literature in the world. Rivarossi's, for example, has 158 pages on N, HO and O gauge trains, all in color. English speakers are lucky in that most manufacturers from countries where other languages are spoken produce editions in English. Before plunging in to buy a model railroad, one might well acquire a few catalogues and spend some time on their perusal at leisure.

Above right: An HO-gauge man's workshop: the beautifully arranged tools used by Paul Huntington of Randolph, Boston, Massachusetts for building his model railroad.

Right: Big machines for big models: a large lathe is used to bore a cylinder in the shop of the Riverside & Great Northern Railroad.

There are numerous periodicals devoted to informing their readers (professional or otherwise) of the principles and practices, old and new, of full-size railroading. These vary from monthlies with general subject matter to quarterlies that specialize. There is one problem that all the periodicals share – how to satisfy both the newcomer who needs articles on basic principles and the old hand who would only be interested in something that represented a pillar of technique. As it is not really satisfactory to produce some sort of compromise, leading magazines such as *Model Railroader* in the United States and *Railway Modeller* in Britain produce booklets and handbooks dealing with basic aspects. The latter's 'Shows You How' series includes such titles as *Building the Baseboard*, *Wiring the Layout* and *Modelling the Landscape*.

From booklets we turn to books and here again a modest selection of what is available would fill a respectable bookcase. A short list is given in the bibliography which includes both the general kind as well as the specialist 'how-to-do-it' sort. Many hobby shops also stock relevant titles in print, while out-of-print ones can usually be borrowed from libraries or bought from

secondhand book dealers such as Norman Kerr (Cartmel, Grange-over-Sands, Lancs, England), Roundhouse Bookshop (High St, Harrow-on-the-Hill, England) or Arnold Joseph (2512 Tratman Avenue, Bronx, New York 10641 USA).

Books on full-size railroads are legion nowadays and of course there are many periodicals too. I was recently asked to suggest those full-size railroad periodicals to whom review copies of a book might be sent; when listed, the total came to 25! This included both Britain and the United States, but was far from exhaustive. Obviously no precise recommendations can be given without exact knowledge of the requirements, but especially recommended are the productions of the Oxford Publishing Co (8 The Roundway, Headington, Oxford). At present their strongest subject is the Great Western Railway, but coverage of other regions of Britain is fast increasing.

The same firm offer another very useful service. They have taken over from British Railways several thousand engineering drawings from the Steam Age and offer them, together with hundreds of old official photographs, to people who want to re-create the

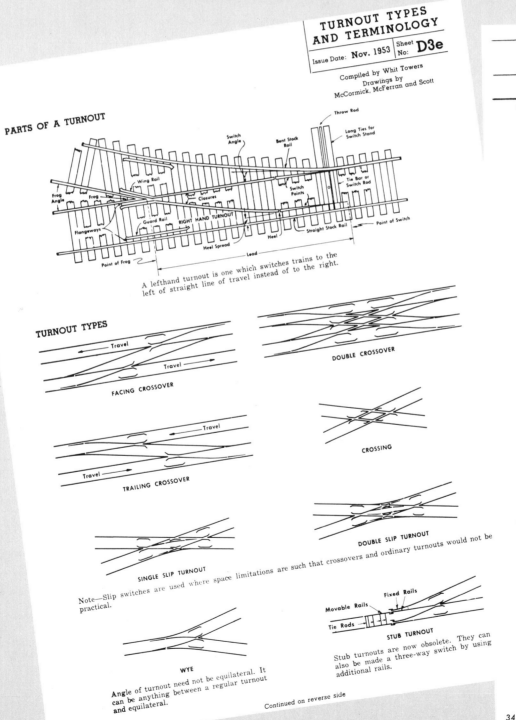

wonderful railroad world that has now completely disappeared. Not only are there drawings and photographs of locomotives available, but also every other imaginable kind of railroad hardware from cattle wagons to signal posts. The National Railway Museum (Leeman Road, York, England) also has similar material in its archives, but it is not yet available to the public.

The whole of Britain is covered by maps to the very large scale of $\frac{1}{2500}$ (almost 25 inches to the mile) and these provide very detailed information on railroad layouts. To this scale the two rails of a railroad line are drawn separately .6mm apart and the positions of such things as signal posts and mileposts can be correctly shown. Stanfords (Long Acre, London WC1, England) can supply these maps. Mr RA Cooke (Evergreen, School Lane, Harwell Village, Oxfordshire OX11 0ES, England) offers layout diagrams of all the railroads in southwest England. His coverage is gradually being extended to the Midlands and no doubt the rest of the country will follow in due course.

If there is a gap in this mass of literature which needs filling, perhaps it lies in books which link the process of seeking out full-size railroad information with its re-creation in miniature. One has recently become available. It is a reprint from the *Model Railroader Magazine* (1027 North Seventh St, Milwaukee, Wisconsin 53233, USA) of a series of articles which appeared under the title 'Modelling the Clinchfield Railroad in N Scale.' The Clinchfield is a real railroad in Kentucky, Virginia and North Carolina, which unusually combines modest size with heavy main-line operations. With the aid of 140 photographs and 65 drawings the book shows how to make a representative model in that very small scale.

In conclusion one can only say that model railroading may not be directly a very useful activity but at least it is a fairly harmless one. Only in fiction does one find little trains used for evil purposes, as in Nicholas Freeling's novel *Gadget* in which the baddies use a model train to assist them in making a do-it-yourself atom bomb. For many people model railroading is a ruling passion and for many more a solace against the problems and pressures of life. Very few indeed are impervious to the lure of railroads, large and small. It is the writer's hope that this book will inspire its readers to do their own thing in model railroads, whether they fit inside a suitcase or cover a tract of countryside.

ould be designed and built to operate satisfactorily at restricted the minimum turnouts and minimum radius curvature speci- operation at typical main line scale speeds (see DATA SHEET ons for one or more higher classes should be used.

'd be designed and built with not less than the specified mini- turnouts for the equipment listed. Use of the largest radius eased (see DATA SHEET D3b, D3c, D3c.1), consistent with tations of the individual layout, is strongly recommended fo

Passenger	Freight
–	
Trailers to 40′ long with full radial couplers	Standard cars to 40′ long with full radial couplers.
Trailers to 50′ long with full radial couplers.	Standard cars to 50′ long with full radial couplers.
Trailers to 60′ long with full radial couplers.	Standard cars to 40′ long with regular couplers.
MU and passenger cars to 60′ long without diaphrams.	Standard cars to 50′ lon with regular couplers.
MU, passenger, postal, baggage cars to 60′ long with diaphrams.	All freight cars.
MU, passenger, postal, baggage cars to 70′ long with diaphrams.	
Old time cars, special short cars to 40′ long without diaphrams.	Standard cars to 40′ with regular couplers
Old time cars, special cars to 50′ long without diaphrams.	Standard cars to 50′ with regular coupler
Old time cars, special cars to 60′ long without diaphrams.	All freight cars.
Suburban, postal and baggage cars to 60′ long with diaphrams.	All freight cars.
Suburban, postal and baggage cars to 70′ long with diaphrams.	
All cars to 80′ long with diaphrams.	
All passenger cars	

/J	F/K	G/L	H/M	N	O
4	5	5	6	6	6
60°	50°	40°	35°	30°	25
00′	118′	146′	166′	193′	23
25″	30″	36½″	41½″	48″	5
19″	22½″	27½″	31″	36″	43
16″	18½″	23″	26″	30½″	36
14″	16½″	20″	23″	26½″	
10″	12″	14½″	16½″	19½″	

crossover should be No. 8. However, for 3-rai of the gap in the third rail.
one class for units with "blind" (flangeless) center wheels in
for operation on sharper curves is not recommended.
ased two classes for articulated locomotives.
tiple Track Centers for various radii.

NMRA BULLETIN

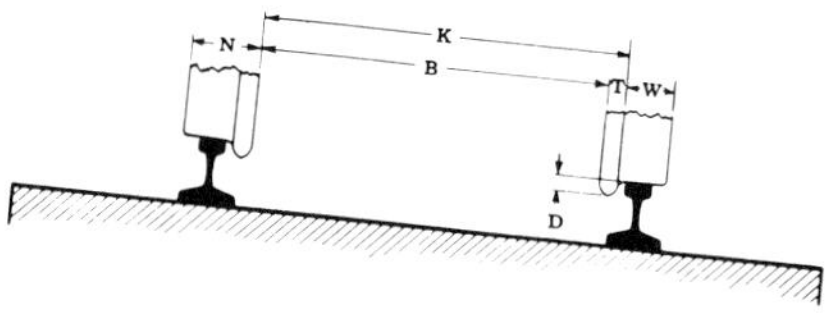

NMRA STANDARDS

WHEELS

Sheet No. S 4 | Revised: Jan. 1974

NAME OF SCALE	K CHECK GAGE (MAX.)	B BACK-TO-BACK OF FLANGES (MIN.)	N TIRE WIDTH (MIN.)	D FLANGE DEPTH (MAX.)
1″ Scale	4.531″ (115.08 mm)	4.375″ (111.13 mm)	.531″ (13.49 mm)	.156″§ (3.96 mm)
¾″ Scale	3.375″ (85.72 mm)	3.250″ (82.56 mm)	.438″ (11.13 mm)	.094″ (2.38 mm)
½″, 17/32″ Scale	2.344″ (59.53 mm)	2.250″ (57.16 mm)	.313″ (7.96 mm)	.062″ (1.57 mm)
No. 1	1.625″ (41.27 mm)	1.552″ (39.43 mm)	.250″ (6.36 mm)	.062″ (1.57 mm)
O. O17	1.172″ (29.76 mm)	1.118″ (28.40 mm)	.172″ (4.37 mm)	.062″ (1.57 mm)
S	.812″ (20.62 mm)	.777″ (19.74 mm)	.124″ (3.15 mm)	.039″ (.99 mm)
OO	.700″ (17.78 mm)	.666″ (16.92 mm)	.108″ (2.75 mm)	.035″ (.88 mm)
HO	.600″ (15.24 mm)	.566″ (14.38 mm)	.108″ (2.75 mm)	.035″ (.88 mm)
TT	.435″ (11.04 mm)	.407″ (10.34 mm)	.077″ (1.96 mm)	.026″ (.66 mm)
On3	.700″ (17.78 mm)	.666″ (16.92 mm)	.124″ (3.15 mm)	.039″ (.99 mm)
On2	.450″ (11.43 mm)	.416″ (10.57 mm)	.108″ (2.75 mm)	.035″ (.88 mm)
HOn3	.373″ (9.47 mm)	.345″ (8.77 mm)	.086″† (2.19 mm)	.026 (.66 mm)
HOn2	.242″ (6.14 mm)	.214″ (5.44 mm)	.077″ (1.95 mm)	.022″ (.55 mm)

†Wheels of STANDARD HO Contour will be permitted.
§For locomotives only. Use .188 Max. (4.78 mm) for tender and car wheels.

Note 1. See RP 25 for recommended wheel contour. Note that maximum flange width T is determined by K minus B (T=K−B).

Note. 2. Tread Width W is determined by N minus T. (See above.)

Note 3. "Wheel Gage" Z, used by some manufacturers, is determined by K plus T.

Note 4. Wheels must have a scale reduction in tread diameter from the prototype.

Note 5. Tread diameters and flanges of wheels in scales smaller than No. 1 must be round, concentric and perpendicular with respect to their axles within 1% TIR (Total Indicator Reading) of the Check Gage distance K, while remaining within the limits of K and B.

Note 6. To avoid difficulty with long wheelbase locomotives in curves sharper than 20° and where guard rails are used on both sides as in special work, the following are suggested:
a. Cut flanges off center drivers
b. Allow lateral movement in driver axles of 1% of the rigid wheelbase length.

JANUARY 1974—SPECIAL ISSUE

21

Bibliography

Ahern, John, *Miniature Building Construction*
  Miniature Landscape Modelling
  Miniature Locomotive Construction
  (all published by Argus Books Ltd)
Beal, Edward, *The Craft of Modelling*
  Railways (Nelson)
  Railway Modelling in Miniature
  (Argus Books Ltd)
Boreham, DA, *Narrow Gauge Railway*
  Modelling (Argus Books Ltd)
Corkhill, WA, *Railway Modelling, An*
  Introduction (David and Charles)
Hambleton, FC, *Locomotives Worth*
  Modelling (Argus Books Ltd)
Hamilton-Ellis, H, *Model Railways, 1838–1939*
  (George Allen & Unwin)
Heywood, Sir Arthur, *Minimum Gauge*
  Railways (Turntable Publications)
Hollingsworth, Brian, *How to Drive a Steam*
  Locomotive (Architectural Press)
Huntley, Ian, *Painting and Lining Models*
  (Argus Books Ltd)
Denkinson, David, *Historic Carriage*
  Drawings (Ian Allan)
Lawrence, Curly (LBSC), *Shops, Shed and*
  Road (Argus Books Ltd)
  Maisie – an LNER 4-4-2, the Words and
  Music (Argus Books Ltd)
Levy, Allen and Whitehouse, Patrick, *The*
  World of Model Trains (Bison Books Ltd)
Model Railroader Staff, *The ABC's of Model*
  Railroading (Kalmbach Books)
  Easy-To-Build Model Railroad Structures
  (Kalmbach Books)
  Railroad Station Planbook
  (Kalmbach Books)
  Scenery for Model Railroads
  (Kalmbach Books)
Morgan, David P, *Model Railroader*
  Cyclopaedia-Steam Locomotives
  (Kalmbach Books)
Roche, FJ, *Historic Locomotive Drawing*
  (Ian Allan)
Shaw, Frederick, *Little Railways of the*
  World (Howell-North)
Tustin, RE, *Garden Model Railways*
  (Argus Books Ltd)

General Railroad Modelling Periodicals:
Live Steam, PO Box 581, Traverse City,
  Michigan 49684, USA
Locomotives Large and Small, Bardonela,
  Adgestone, Sandown, Isle of Wight,
  England
Model Engineer, PO Box 35, Hemel
  Hempstead, Herts HP1 1EE, England
Model Railroader, 1027 North Seventh St,
  Milwaukee, Wisconsin 53233, USA
Model Railway Constructor, Terminal House,
  Shepperton TW17 8AS, England
Model Railways, 12 Bridge St, Hemel
  Hempstead, Herts HP1 1EE, England
Railroad Model Craftsman, PO Box 700,
  Newton, New Jersey 07860, USA
Railroad Modeller, 7950 Deering Avenue,
  Canoga Park, California 91304, USA
Railway Modeller, Peco Publications Ltd,
  Beer, Seaton, Devon EX12 3NA, England

Index

Picture Credits